"*When Your Teen Has an Eating Disorder* is an outstanding resource for parents who are confronted with the various challenges that come their way when their child has an eating disorder. This book provides parents with a ringing endorsement that *they* are the ones who should take center stage in their child's treatment, and that it is the parents who ultimately will be instrumental in bringing about recovery for their child. Muhlheim's depth of experience working with such families shines through in this practical guide of how to make sense of the everyday challenges that a diagnosis of an eating disorder brings to such families. Most important, this book provides parents with a steady dose of practical strategies to employ while engaged in family-based treatment (FBT), and thereby adds a critical resource in this struggle to overcome their child's illness."

—**Daniel Le Grange, PhD**, codeveloper of FBT; Benioff UCSF professor in children's health and eating disorders; director in the department of psychiatry at the University of California, San Francisco; and coauthor of *Help Your Teenager Beat an Eating Disorder* and *Treatment Manual for Anorexia Nervosa*

"This book fills a necessary gap in helping parents to feel effective and engaged in tackling their child's eating disorder. The calm, compassionate voice of Lauren Muhlheim describing the challenges and engagement associated with family-based re-nourishment provides a necessary succor for families engaging in FBT. Her commonsense, easy-to-read, and insightful book is like having a seasoned FBT therapist on speed dial. Muhlheim's work with families, as well as her keen interest in and development of FBT practice for therapists, coalesce into this great book."

—**Kathleen Kara Fitzpatrick, PhD**, psychologist and director of the Outpatient Eating Disorder Clinic in the department of child and adolescent psychiatry and behavioral sciences at Stanford University and Stanford Children's Hospital

"Eating disorders are serious diseases that can have a major impact on the physical and mental health of those affected. They can easily go unrecognized and untreated. In her book, eating disorders expert Lauren Muhlheim helps readers become fully aware of practical strategies and helpful tips to apply FBT—the only evidence-based treatment for adolescents with eating disorders. As Lauren states, a parent's involvement and understanding is crucial for better outcomes. This is a book that is worth reading, and I am sure many parents and families will benefit greatly. I loved it and I give my most enthusiastic applause for this addition to the eating disorders literature!"

> —**Eva Maria Trujillo Chi Vacuán, MD**, past president at the Academy for Eating Disorders; medical director and founder of Comenzar de Nuevo, A.C., International Treatment Center for Eating Disorders; clinical professor at Tecnológico de Monterrey School of Medicine

"In this groundbreaking book, Lauren Muhlheim provides a wise, inspiring, and compassionate guide through the complicated journey of an eating disorder. *When Your Teen Has an Eating Disorder* is a must-read for anyone who cares for a young person suffering with disordered eating and negative body image. Above all, this book provides true hope that healing does indeed happen!"

> —**Jenni Schaefer**, author of *Life Without Ed*; *Almost Anorexic*; and *Goodbye Ed, Hello Me*

"This outstanding book concisely and methodically takes you through the steps needed to treat your teen's eating disorder. Everything parents absolutely must know is in here. Lauren Muhlheim is an experienced clinician who really understands the practicalities of what happens at home."

> —**Eva Musby**, parent and author of *Anorexia and Other Eating Disorders*

"*When Your Teen Has an Eating Disorder* is an absolute must-read for parents who would like to support their child's recovery at home. This validating and accessible self-help guide walks parents through the most evidence-based treatment approach for child and adolescent eating disorders—FBT. The detailed case examples, step-by-step action plans, and helpful worksheets bring FBT to life and demonstrate exactly how parents can implement its useful and timely strategies calmly and confidently at the very next meal."

—**Jennifer J. Thomas, PhD**, codirector of the Eating Disorders Clinical and Research Program, Massachusetts General Hospital; associate professor of psychology in the department of psychiatry, Harvard Medical School; and author of *Almost Anorexic*

"Lauren Muhlheim's book walks readers through the terrifying terrain of helping a teen recover from an eating disorder. She offers evidence-based information and practical advice in a reassuring, matter-of-fact tone, which is exactly what parents need when they're in the thick of a child's illness."

—**Harriet Brown**, author of *Shadow Daughter*, *Body of Truth*, and *Brave Girl Eating*; professor of magazine journalism, S.I. Newhouse School of Public Communications

"This is the best workbook for parents that I have reviewed. Muhlheim does an outstanding job of emphasizing the importance of parents in the recovery process and offers evidence-based, practical advice on how to accomplish recovery. This is the book that I will recommend to families as an introduction to the illnesses and what the challenges of recovery will be.... Excellent contribution to the field."

> —**Craig Johnson, PhD, CEDS, FAED**, chief science officer and codirector of the Family Institute, Eating Recovery Center; clinical professor of psychiatry, University of Oklahoma College of Medicine

"*When Your Teen Has an Eating Disorder* empowers readers with practical information and evidence-based tools for navigating these illnesses as a family. It's a hopeful, helpful guide written with the understanding that parents truly are on the front lines of eating disorder recovery."

> —**Claire Mysko**, chief executive officer, National Eating Disorders Association

"Any parent with a loved one suffering from an eating disorder, as well as clinicians treating them, will benefit from this treasure. As a clinical psychologist devoting my career to including families as part of the treatment team, I strongly recommend this book to help you navigate best practices to restore your loved one to health."

> —**Roxanne E. Rockwell, PhD**, director, adolescent eating disorders services, Eating Disorders Center for Treatment and Research, USA; assistant clinical professor, UC San Diego department of psychiatry, School of Medicine

"This is an outstanding, practical guide that can help any parent or caregiver navigate the daunting terrain of helping their loved one fight an eating disorder, and one of the best books out there. To parents looking for a guide: pick this one up, read it, and move forward with renewed confidence that you are not alone. Hear the voices of other parents who have been through this. You've got this, and Lauren Muhlheim is there to make sure you know you are your child's greatest asset in fighting this disease."

—**Rebecka Peebles, MD**, director of research and quality innovations, Eating Disorder Assessment and Treatment Program, The Children's Hospital of Philadelphia; assistant professor, The Craig-Dalsimer Division of Adolescent Medicine; department of pediatrics, Perelman School of Medicine at the University of Pennsylvania

"Lauren Muhlheim offers a practical, accessible guide to helping your teen recover from an eating disorder. Her book offers step-by-step guidance on how to manage meals, as well as the emotions and conversations that occur around food. More, she provides hope that teens *can* recover, and empowers families to facilitate the healing at home."

—**Stacey Rosenfeld, PhD**, psychologist, certified group psychotherapist, certified eating disorders specialist, and author of *Does Every Woman Have an Eating Disorder?*

When Your
Teen Has
an Eating
Disorder

. . .

Practical Strategies to
Help Your Teen Recover from
Anorexia, Bulimia & Binge Eating

LAUREN MUHLHEIM, PsyD

New Harbinger Publications, Inc.

Publisher's Note

This publication is designed to provide accurate and authoritative information in regard to the subject matter covered. It is sold with the understanding that the publisher is not engaged in rendering psychological, financial, legal, or other professional services. If expert assistance or counseling is needed, the services of a competent professional should be sought.

NEW HARBINGER PUBLICATIONS is a registered trademark of New Harbinger Publications, Inc.

Distributed in Canada by Raincoast Books

Copyright © 2018 by Lauren Muhlheim
                  New Harbinger Publications, Inc.
                  5674 Shattuck Avenue
                  Oakland, CA 94609
                  www.newharbinger.com

Cover design by Amy Shoup

Acquired by Elizabeth Hollis Hansen

Edited by Marisa Solís

All Rights Reserved

Library of Congress Cataloging-in-Publication Data on file

Printed in the United States of America

23   22   21

10   9   8   7   6   5   4

Contents

Foreword

As a parent whose precious child was almost killed by an eating disorder, I know the emotional impact an eating disorder can have on the entire family. Today our daughter is alive and thriving. I'm an advocate now, and I have spent years talking to policy-makers, clinicians, researchers, and families affected by mental health crises. When I speak with a parent, we don't discuss the science or statistics or theory. We talk about that one precious son or daughter—about that very day, and that next meal, and keeping the whole family afloat when time, money, and hope are in short supply.

This book is about that moment in your life—and about your family and your suffering loved one. All the theory and policy and data are useless and of little interest when you are living with constant struggle and being haunted by genuine fears for the life of a young person in your care.

If you are a parent picking up this book, you are likely facing a daily struggle and in need of direction and practical ideas from a trustworthy source. You are looking for problem solving and for clues that this will be a useful investment of your time and trust. You are looking for a resource that helps you in the real world, where families may not have cutting-edge clinical support and a knowledgeable community. You need help today, not next week or next month. I have been there. I have two shelves of eating disorder books for parents written during the past thirty years. I have even met and talked with most of the authors. And although all my dog-eared copies contain numerous pearls of wisdom, none of them contains all the pearls in one publication.

What has been missing is a book that puts the practical and the best available science in one place. This is that book. *When Your Teen Has an Eating Disorder* is about *your* teen. In this year. In your care.

Your quest to understand the illness—and to be the most effective parent while you support your child to recovery—is some of the best parenting you will ever need to do. It's hard, but no one promised you that parenting would be easy. It's also confusing, but not too much for you to handle. Just as you found your way through teething and toddlerhood with your unique little person, you will find your family's unique way through this.

Your solutions will not be exactly like anyone else's. That is why Lauren Muhlheim's approach works. Instead of being given prescriptions and directives, you will be empowered to choose solutions that work for you and your family. Instead of blaming you or your child for the problem, she sees you as the most important element of the recovery journey.

It is a journey. As a parent who has been there and known countless families around the world who have faced an eating disorder, I wish I could give you a map with a straight line to success—but your path will reflect your family's strengths, history, and values. I wish I could assure you of success, but that is for you to both define and to own. Families struggle, stumble, and get back up again. Not all are successful, but that is why the tools you choose and the loving commitment and energy you put into the journey matter.

There will be voices in your ear—you may have heard them already—promising easy and definitive answers. You will hear attractive solutions that align with your beliefs and your fears. You may be tempted to choose the most expensive option, thinking it is likely to be the most effective; or the closest to home, because you want to keep life normal; or the one that promises the fastest results, because you think you can't bear any more resistance, disruption, or uncertainty. You may even be considering an option that takes you out of the picture for a while, and the problem out of the house. But if you look at the data, and you talk with researchers and successful families, it is clear that the best place to recover is at home, the best daily providers are family, and the best professional supports utilize modern methods backed by research.

This book is the tool I will be giving parents, because Muhlheim's approach as a therapist, writer, and leader in our field is empowering to all of us. You will find her to be a clear and respected collaborator as you work with your own treatment providers, family members, and support team. She is practical, she is evidence-based, and she believes in the power and loving commitment of parents.

"Parents are my best teachers," Muhlheim says. Families benefit from an approach that is informed by and celebrates the wisdom of families. Not all of us are fortunate enough to have a clinical team that is up to date on best practices and thinks parents are central to treatment, but you deserve that and can find it in this book. You can share the strategies in this book with your providers, and you can demonstrate your courage and commitment to being a major part of the solution.

Muhlheim brings you onto the treatment team and regards you as a collaborative team player. She shares her clinical insights and the stories of families she has known. She addresses you directly, with respect for both your commitment and your skills.

She believes in *you*, as do I. You are not alone. The tools and tips and perspectives in this book will be steady companions as you do some of the most important parenting of your life!

—Laura Collins Lyster-Mensh
Author and Advocate
Warrenton, Virginia
February 2018

Introduction

If you've picked up this book, your teen has likely been diagnosed with an eating disorder. If your teen has not been diagnosed, but you are concerned enough to be reading this, something is probably going on. You may recognize the need for your teen to gain weight but can't figure out how to get her to eat. Maybe your teen is engaging in unhealthy behaviors—such as severe dieting, bingeing, purging, and excessive exercise—that you don't know how to address. Or perhaps your teen is in an eating disorder treatment program that excludes you from the treatment altogether and you want to be more involved. You are probably feeling scared, confused, and overwhelmed.

The good news is that you *can* confront the eating disorder—*as a family*. Not only does this better empower you, the parent, it is actually the most effective way to tackle an eating disorder. My ten years as a therapist for families facing eating disorders have convinced me that treatments in which parents play a central role offer the greatest— maybe the *only*—chance for your teen's full recovery. There are many ways to support your child. In this book, I will teach you how to put your love into action and feed your child back to health.

A Few Words on This Book's Terminology

When I refer to "parent," I mean it to include caregivers and legal guardians. When I refer to your teenage child, I use the words "teen" and "child" interchangeably.

Family-Based Treatment

It can be difficult to know who to turn to for help. Many communities lack knowledgeable, skilled providers. You may be told that your child's refusal to eat is just a phase and to return only if she gets worse. You may be encouraged to send your teen away for more intensive treatment. You may be given conflicting advice and don't know what to do.

However, it's been my experience that waiting for your teen to worsen, or being intentionally left out of the treatment plan, is ill advised. What *does* work is putting parents in a highly supportive role as soon as possible.

Research demonstrates that parents can powerfully support their teen during the years it can take to recover from an eating disorder. This model of care diverges from the traditional, individually focused therapeutic approach. A family-centered approach immediately targets malnutrition and problematic behaviors, and it offers parents the opportunity to help their teen recover faster and more completely (Lock et al. 2010).

This book is based on the leading treatment from this school of thought: *family-based treatment (FBT)*. This approach empowers parents to oversee renourishment and remain embedded throughout the entire treatment process. FBT has become the leading treatment for child and teen eating disorders—including anorexia nervosa, bulimia nervosa, and atypical and subthreshold eating disorders—because it places *you* at the helm of recovery, driving your teen toward healthy eating and other recovery-consistent behaviors. FBT represents an about-face from traditional treatments that blame and exclude parents.

Act Now

In my practice, parents sometimes want to take a wait-and-see approach. Or they worry that prematurely taking charge will make things worse. I have even heard pediatricians advise parents, "FBT is too extreme at this point. Why don't you wait a few months?"

But in my eight years practicing FBT, I have seen no case in which parents aggravated a potential eating disorder by drawing attention to it. I have never met a parent who regretted intervening—only parents who regretted their hesitation. Even if your teen's eating disorder seems mild, or you aren't sure he has one, I encourage you to make resolving the problem a priority. Not doing so can risk your child's future. Some teens die from eating disorders and others remain ill for decades (Arcelus et al. 2011; Eddy et al. 2017). The window of opportunity is finite, and undertreatment at the onset worsens the prognosis for a disorder that can become chronic or fatal. Early intervention drives superior outcomes.

Dieting and other eating disorder behaviors are reinforced through repetition and become more ingrained over time. Allowing these behaviors to run their course without interruption makes them harder to break. The longer someone with an eating disorder engages in behaviors, the greater the risk for permanent damage. So don't delay; seek help for your child right away.

Stay Committed

Plan to stay committed for as long as it takes. Eating disorder recovery respects no set timeline. Full recovery requires time: eating enough food regularly throughout the day, maintaining a healthy weight, and refraining from restricting, bingeing, purging, and excessive exercise for an extended span—in most cases for *years*.

Whichever type of treatment your teen receives, there is always room for parents to provide meal support and encourage recovery behaviors. The work I prescribe for you will be hard and require focus. It will demand a big time and energy commitment. You will be doing work that, at a treatment center, would be performed by trained professionals. Prioritizing the eating disorder may mean putting you and your child's lives on hold. Some parents may need to take time off work or postpone vacation plans. Extended family members may need to play a supportive role. Some young adults may need to delay going to college.

Putting recovery above all else can be a struggle. You may have trips or other family objectives planned. You may fear that canceling an activity will disappoint your sick teen or her sibling. But consider this: if your child had diabetes or cancer, how would you prioritize her treatment versus other family activities? An eating disorder can be just as deadly as these better-understood disorders.

You hold your teen's fate in your hands. You must persist in making recovery a priority.

Don't Wait for Your Teen to Want Help

Accept that your child may reject your involvement in treatment, your management of his eating, or even receiving any treatment at all. This is common. Many parents who want to allow their child a role in his own recovery may be tempted to delay treatment until he is willing. But without intervention, that willingness may never develop!

I believe that the research on the efficacy of FBT suggests that waiting for teens to want help is a mistake. You, the parent, can be a change agent. You must act on your child's behalf and seek treatment for him, especially if he is under eighteen. At this age, most teens are neither emotionally nor cognitively able to make good decisions regarding recovery. Your teen still lives under your roof—capitalize on this opportunity to act now. An eating disorder can tighten its grip once a young adult moves out. Many adults with eating disorders had teenage onsets that were inadequately treated.

Take your teenager to a professional to receive a formal diagnosis and rule out other medical explanations. If practical in your area, ensure that the professional is an eating disorder expert or, at a minimum, takes your concern seriously. However, if the professional reassures you that everything is okay but you still feel that something is amiss, don't settle. Even medical professionals commonly miss the early signs of an eating disorder.

Why I Wrote This Book

I am a clinical psychologist, an eating disorder specialist, and the mother of teens and young adults. During graduate school I trained in a bulimia research lab. This work profoundly influenced me, and I have remained close to the research world ever since. We clinicians deliver the best treatment for specific conditions when we consult the research.

While working in China in 2010, I encountered teens whose treatment at inpatient clinics meant sending them to the United States or Australia, a whole continent away from their parents. Desperate for a solution that honored the family bond, I began my training in family-based treatment (FBT).

The FBT therapist's role is to empower parents to manage their child's recovery. The therapist's stance is encouraging but not prescriptive—not telling parents exactly how to accomplish the mission but coaching them to problem-solve. There is a shortage of appropriately trained professionals to guide the number of families needing help with this approach. Until recently, little written material about this process has existed. Several online parent forums and organizations have formed to provide assistance, but there remains a lack of formal parent resources.

As a mother, I can relate to parents' terror in dealing with these devastating illnesses. Empowering families to help their children recover, rather than sending them away to be "fixed" by someone else, is my work's greatest reward. I have worked extensively with parents of teens with eating disorders and know their concerns about helping their children. I have also worked with entire treatment teams including medical professionals and registered dieticians.

My work today is dedicated to empowering parents. My passion is providing parents the tools and evidence-based principles to help their teens heal.

Who This Book Is For

The program outlined in this book, based on FBT, will provide the tools to help your child and family reclaim your lives. As loving parents, you are uniquely qualified for this job.

Specifically, this book is aimed at you if one of the following is true:

- **You have no reliable access to treatment and are looking to help your teen recover without the help of specialists**. Many parents attempt to help their teen recover on his own without appropriate therapeutic guidance. This book attempts to bridge the gap for families living in areas with limited treatment options.

- **Your teen is in a non-FBT treatment.** I believe you can still provide meal support and structure to support your teen's recovery (but please discuss this with your treatment team!).

- **Your teen is already in FBT and you want to supplement it with additional knowledge and guidance.**

Parents might be able to begin the process of restoring a teen's nutrition and eating patterns to optimal levels without a therapist's involvement, but more intense or challenging symptoms may require expert care. At a minimum, your teen should be examined and seen regularly by a medical doctor to monitor for serious medical complications, a discussion of which is beyond this book's scope.

This book's strategies may help parents of teens with any of the following: anorexia nervosa, bulimia nervosa, other specified feeding or eating disorder (OSFED), subclinical disordered eating, and, in some cases, avoidant/restrictive food intake disorder (ARFID). The binge cessation strategies can also be applied to binge eating disorder.

If an eating disorder is wearing you down, or you have been instructed to step back by well-meaning but poorly informed professionals, this book is designed to reinstate you to your fundamental job of parenting, because your child needs you now more than ever. This book makes uncommon offers: the permission to take an active approach, and the tools with which to do so.

What This Book Will Cover

I survey the different eating disorders and the mechanisms that maintain them. I discuss the benefits of a parent-supported approach and recount cases of parents who helped their teen recover. I address target weight establishment based on childhood growth patterns; meal plan implementation; increasing the caloric density of meals; planning, supervising, and delivering meals; and supporting children to consume the food you provide. I suggest incentives to get your teen to eat as well as how to limit other behaviors, such as exercise, bingeing, and vomiting. I also include suggestions for maintaining calm during mealtimes in the presence of an escalating teen. I cover coping skills for parents and teens; food flexibility expansion and eating behavior generalization to other settings; returning control to and helping your child with the development of independent and intuitive eating; how to deal with special situations like travel and college; and relapse prevention.

The strategies I provide in this book are derived primarily from FBT for eating disorders, with input from cognitive-behavioral therapy (CBT, the leading eating disorder treatment for adults) and my clinical experience. This book offers parents practical suggestions and an array of options for returning your teen to optimal health. There are many ways to support your teen. No single method works for all families. The only course parents should avoid is to *do nothing.*

Expect this to be difficult. Specifically, you will be asked to plan and prepare meals—and eat with your teen—for as long as it takes for your teen to be able to eat independently without eating disorder behaviors. The process you will undertake is akin to running a residential treatment center in your house. It can involve supervising your teen between meals and, in some cases, around the clock. FBT includes the gradual return of control to the teen in a way that supports her long-term recovery. Along the way, you may need to examine your own beliefs about healthy eating and weight.

This is what success can look like:

- Your teen has ceased to exercise excessively, is eating healthy amounts for his growth, and has reengaged in moderate sports participation.

- Your teen is no longer a regular emergency room visitor with an unstable heart rate; he maintains a healthy weight with minimal meal supervision.

- Your young adult is in college 3,000 miles away, eating regularly and independently while in remission from the eating disorder.

I believe in parental intuition. My intention is to arm you with knowledge to inform this instinct and empower you to act.

Feed, Love, Heal

Feeding and helping your teen recover are acts of love. However, love is not always easy or gentle. The strength and resolve you show will bring your teen back to health. There will be stress and challenges, and I will offer suggestions for managing those. This is not going to be easy, but it will be one of the most rewarding things you will ever do as a parent.

Online Materials

At this book's website (http://www.newharbinger.com/40439), I provide free supplemental materials, including forms and worksheets, to help you think through the application of the strategies I share in this manuscript. Discussions of specialized topics and additional resources may also be found there. (See the very back of this book for details on how to access the site.) References to these materials will appear in boxes like this one.

CHAPTER 1

What's Happening to My Teen?

In this chapter, I'll walk you through some background information that will help you better understand eating disorders and how they may affect your child. You'll be given tools to assess whether you are facing a problem and learn concepts that will help you to help your teen recover.

The Nine Truths About Eating Disorders

Some myths about eating disorders are so widespread that the eating disorders advocacy community has created a consensus document, *Nine Truths About Eating Disorders*. Please refer to http://www.newharbinger.com/40439 for information about the truths.

Meet some teenagers with eating disorders whose families supported them in their recovery:

Valentina, twelve, had been considered "slightly overweight" prior to a growth spurt. Her weight remained stable, but she grew several inches. Over time she became obsessed with her weight, reading food labels, eating minuscule meals, and avoiding starches. Valentina began exercising and criticized her old eating habits and those of her classmates. She began to avoid rice, a family staple. In two months, her weight plummeted. Alarmed by her weight loss, her parents encouraged her to eat more, explaining it was for her health. Valentina told them she got full quickly and refused to eat more.

Oscar, fifteen, became more restrictive in his eating and obsessed with building muscle. He said he wanted "six-pack abs." He started doing sit-ups and push-ups, running, and throwing up after meals. He wore extra layers of clothing to encourage sweating, which he hoped would increase weight loss. Oscar frequently checked his physique in the mirror. He lost weight while growing. He was especially frightened of fried foods, believing any fat he ingested would show on his body.

Susan, sixteen, swam on her high school and club teams. One teammate often threw up due to the intensity of the practices. Susan feared that she too would start to throw up and began refusing to eat dinner prior to practice. When Susan returned home after practice she wasn't hungry. Over the course of a few months she lost several pounds. Her period stopped. As her fear of vomiting increased, her eating became increasingly restrictive.

Karen, seventeen, taught yoga and insisted on vegetarianism and "clean eating." She appeared to be living a healthy lifestyle, but parents discovered from her worried friends that she was bingeing and purging.

Do any of these stories feel familiar? They illustrate just some of the many ways that eating disorders may present in a teen.

You may not even be sure your child has an eating disorder. But maybe you have observed strange behavior at meals. Maybe your teen has become extremely picky about what she is eating. Maybe your teen is obsessed with food labels or watching the Food Channel. Maybe your child has lost a lot of weight but is not skinny. Maybe you have a son and wonder whether it's even possible for a boy to have an eating disorder.

How do you know how seriously to take this?

Types of Eating Disorders

There are several types of eating disorders. What follows are descriptions of the major diagnoses, based on the *Diagnostic and Statistical Manual of Mental Health Disorders*, fifth edition (DSM-5; American Psychiatric Association 2013). Most real-world eating disorders do not fall neatly into a single category. A patient often exhibits signs of more than one disorder either at different times or concurrently. Yet these disorders share broad similarities in the dangers they pose to the individuals and the treatments that are effective.

Be aware that eating disorder symptoms may fluctuate over time. The specific eating disorder identified may even change, a phenomenon that researchers call "diagnostic crossover"—for example, one-third of patients with anorexia nervosa will eventually develop bulimia nervosa (Eddy et al. 2008).

Tragically, misinformation about eating disorders abounds even among medical professionals, who usually receive little training in eating disorders (Mahr et al. 2015). Missed opportunities for diagnosis are common during the early course of a young person's eating disorder. If a clinical diagnosis is negative and your gut says otherwise, follow your gut. The sooner your teen gets help, the better.

Binge Eating Disorder

Binge eating disorder (BED) is the most recently recognized eating disorder and the one most common among adults and males. Individuals with BED engage in episodes of eating large amounts of food in a short period of time, usually accompanied by feeling out of control. For example, they may eat a box of cookies or several containers of ice cream in one sitting. Individuals with BED usually think constantly about dieting while feeling a compulsion to binge eat. This compulsion is coupled with anxiety, shame, disgust, guilt, and self-criticism around eating.

While BED is found in higher rates among people of larger body size, it can be found in people with bodies of any size. Individuals with binge eating disorder may start each day as if they are on a diet, but they break all their diet rules by the end of the day.

Bulimia Nervosa

Bulimia nervosa involves obsessive and irrational thoughts about the body, food, and exercise. People with bulimia nervosa will repeatedly start a diet but then "blow it" and surrender to compulsions to binge eat. Binges often result from the pressure created by setting rigid rules against eating certain "forbidden" foods, such as desserts. These foods become irresistible; the individual violates the rule and binges. The distress over having "overeaten" is followed by behaviors designed to compensate: vomiting, fasting, excessive exercise, and laxative and diuretic use. Those with bulimia nervosa may show only one or multiple types of these behaviors.

Anorexia Nervosa

Individuals with anorexia nervosa have a distorted view of their bodies, obsessive and illogical thoughts about food and exercise, and fear around the act of eating. They have an irrational fear of weight gain and eat too little, which causes an unnaturally low body weight for the individual. In the stereotypical presentation, those with anorexia nervosa maintain a dangerously low weight, but anorexia nervosa can also be diagnosed in individuals with larger bodies who have lost significant weight. People with anorexia nervosa eat a narrow range of foods and exhibit extreme anxiety around eating higher-calorie foods.

Avoidant/Restrictive Food Intake Disorder

Avoidant/restrictive food intake disorder (ARFID) includes those who eat too little to maintain their nutritional needs but do not have the body image concerns commonly seen in anorexia nervosa. They may be "willing" to increase weight but remain terrified of eating. Individuals with ARFID often refuse food but not usually the same types of foods typically feared by patients afraid of weight gain. They may have been fussy eaters with a sensory sensitivity (such as a difficulty with certain textures of foods) that began in early childhood. The designation also includes people who do not eat because they are fearful of vomiting. This disorder is more common in children and teens than in adults.

Other Specified Feeding and Eating Disorder

Other specified feeding and eating disorder (OSFED) is a catchall comprising a spectrum of eating problems that cause distress and impairment but fail to meet the specific criteria for anorexia nervosa, bulimia nervosa, or binge eating disorder. OSFED may be referred to as a "subclinical eating disorder," meaning the person does not meet full criteria for one of the other disorders. Even so, this diagnosis should be taken seriously—research shows that many of these people will go on to develop full eating disorders.

People with OSFED may have isolated symptoms of multiple disorders, or fall just short of meeting the criteria for a single disorder. For example, individuals diagnosed with OSFED may not binge or purge frequently enough to qualify for a diagnosis of bulimia nervosa or binge eating disorder, but they may be mentally preoccupied with thoughts about weight and food. They may have a purging disorder without any bingeing behavior. Or they may engage in night eating, a variant of binge eating disorder characterized by eating late at night and a parallel disruption to sleep patterns. Despite a less well-defined set of symptoms, these people may still suffer greatly.

OSFED can also describe a recovery phase that many people pass through on their way from one of the other eating disorders to full recovery.

Related Diagnoses

In addition to the major diagnoses, there are two diagnoses that may describe your teen.

Orthorexia Nervosa

Orthorexia nervosa is not an accepted eating disorder according to the DSM-5, although recently it has attracted significant attention as a proposed diagnosis. It involves adhering to a theory and practice of healthy eating so strictly that one's health, school, work, or social life suffers. It has many similarities to anorexia nervosa and is treated similarly. The primary difference is that a person with orthorexia restricts food in order to be healthy rather than to control shape or weight. Orthorexia typically begins as an interest in healthy eating that escalates and becomes compulsive. Over time, the person's preoccupation with healthy eating intensifies and squeezes out other interests.

Muscle Dysmorphia

Muscle dysmorphia is a body dysmorphic disorder (itself a form of obsessive-compulsive disorder or OCD) that some researchers believe is really a manifestation of anorexia nervosa that is more common in males (Griffiths, Murray, and Touyz 2013). While people with muscle dysmorphia may have similarly rigid thoughts about food and body, they desire a bigger and more muscular body, rather than the thinness associated with traditional anorexia nervosa. Consequently, people with muscle dysmorphia are more likely to focus on weight lifting, eating high-protein foods to build muscle, and using supplements or steroids. It is believed that a large percentage of body builders may have muscle dysmorphia.

Co-occurring Disorders

Eating disorders in youth commonly occur alongside other mental health disorders. Children with eating disorders may exhibit depression, anxiety, OCD, post-traumatic stress disorder (PTSD), personality disorders, substance use disorders, and self-injurious behaviors (Campbell and Peebles 2014). These other disorders may either precede or coexist with the eating disorder. Treating such problems is beyond the scope of this book; however, I implore you to address the eating disorder with all possible urgency, despite accompanying problems. In fact, I would argue that short of serious self-harm behavior, restoring optimal brain health via proper nutrition should be your top priority. It is possible that some of these other problems may improve as your teen's nutrition and eating patterns return to optimal levels (Accurso et al. 2014; Keys, Brozek, and Henschel 1950).

How Do I Know If My Child Has a Problem?

Now that you have learned about the types of eating disorders, your next question is presumably how to determine whether your child has one. Eating disorders can be cunning. If eating behaviors are a continuum with "harmless" at one end and "disordered" at the other, a broad range in the middle could be considered "normal." Every teen's "normal" is different. One key thing to assess is any *change* from your child's previous behaviors.

What Do Healthy Teen Eating and Exercise Look Like?

For parents immersed in a culture that values thinness and promotes dieting as "normal," it can be hard to recognize normal eating and exercise behaviors. Popular media coverage of celebrities' diets, along with weight-loss competition television shows, normalize extreme exercise, restrictive eating, and other unhealthy behaviors.

Bodies are meant to be diverse, and teens can be healthy at various sizes and shapes. A healthy developing teen experiences sustained growth and weight gain, with spurts in both height and weight during puberty. Appetite level varies among individuals, but in normally developing teens there is no obsessive thinking about food. Normally developing teens may take food to their room, but they'll also eat comfortably in the presence of others. They can eat with ease in different settings—at home, at restaurants, and so on. Their food intake may vary considerably by meal—some days, they may be naturally hungrier than others. Overall, healthy teens eat an amount that seems proportionate to their activity. They may be picky about some foods, more often vegetables, less often starches, meat, or fats. They can make food selections without much difficulty.

Other normal behaviors: Healthy teens use condiments. They like a range of foods and eat them when made available. They make food requests. They get hungry and will ask what's for dinner. Healthy teens look forward to desserts. They are rarely excessively cranky and don't skip meals. They get themselves food on an as-wanted or as-needed basis. They won't often talk about dieting or the health value of foods or read food labels. While healthy teens may be anxious about their appearance, they don't weigh themselves or worry about their weight. They don't run to the bathroom right after every meal. They appear calm after eating.

Most normally developing teens don't obsess about exercise. If they do, it is usually in the context of sports participation. Most are not usually very disciplined or rigorous in training outside of organized practice. They can sit still and be restful. Exercise is not expressed as an attempt to counteract the effects of eating.

What Do Teen Eating Disorders Look Like?

Children and younger teens may not display the more stereotypical signs of an eating disorder that are seen in older patients. For example, younger patients are less likely to binge eat or to know about or obtain things like diet pills or laxatives. Bulimia nervosa and associated behaviors tend to (but do not always!) have a later age of onset.

So, what are some of the warning signs to which parents need to be attuned?

Weight Loss, Lack of Weight Gain, or Lack of Growth

A common sign of an eating disorder is weight loss—intentional or not—or weighing less than is optimal based on your teen's growth patterns over the years. However, children and teens may not actually lose weight when they develop an eating disorder. Instead, they may fail to grow or gain weight *as expected*. While your pediatrician should be able to catch this, not all pediatricians are trained in spotting eating disorders. This can lead to a missed diagnosis. **Tip:** it is important to compare height and weight against your child's own past growth records. You'll learn how to do this in chapter 3.

Eating Less or Eating a Narrower Range of Foods

Your teen may have gone vegetarian; started a weight-loss, raw food, whole food, or "clean" diet; abandoned red meat or desserts; or started to count calories. In some cases, eating restrictions may appear unintentional. Younger teens and children are less likely to engage in goal-directed dieting—they more often subtly resist eating enough to maintain weight gain and growth. Their portions may seem unusually small.

Parents usually observe an expanding list of rejected foods that were previously eaten. Some excuses teens give for not eating foods they liked include not being hungry or having vague health goals (which parents may often support at first). Teens may complain of stomachaches or seem to get full very easily.

Excessive Exercise, Hyperactivity, or Restlessness

Your teen may have become preoccupied with exercise. He may spend hours at the gym, do jumping jacks in his room, do sit-ups while watching television, or run laps around the neighborhood. Your teen may engage in exercise to "burn off" dessert consumed the night before or in anticipation of eating at a party. He may even abandon other activities in order to exercise or appear obsessive about his sports participation and request extra training. In some cases, teens will attempt to burn calories by standing when they could sit, or finding ways to walk more, even at home.

In younger teens, the activity may be less goal-directed; they may appear restless or hyperactive and may move around in an unintentional way. Parents often report that their children fidget or stand all the time. They may be unable to be still in normally tranquil contexts, such as while watching television. This behavior may look more like attention deficit/hyperactivity disorder (ADHD), so parents may not realize that an eating disorder could be an explanation (O'Toole 2013).

Increased Interest in Cooking or Watching Cooking Shows

Your teen's interest in cooking may have suddenly increased. Contrary to both popular belief and what they themselves verbalize, people with restrictive eating disorders do not lack an appetite. In fact, they are often ravenous and thinking about food. Someone of any age with an eating disorder may collect recipes and even cook for others—but then refuse to eat the meal she prepared.

A restrictive eater may have a similar preoccupation with watching cooking shows on TV. One teen obsessively watched *Cupcake Wars* for hours a day to the exclusion of other activities. Parents often interpret a teen's interest in food as a good thing. However, be aware that this "interest" may be a redirection of the hunger drive. People who are not eating enough obsess about food. That is why teens with restrictive eating may displace eating with other food-oriented activities.

Binge Eating, Self-Induced Vomiting, Laxative or Diuretic Use, or Cleanses

These behaviors are never considered normal and are clear warning signs. The behaviors may be hidden from parents, but parents may see traces. Your teen may run to the bathroom or take long showers shortly after meals. He may skip breakfast and lunch so he can eat more at dinner. You may notice that food (especially high-carbohydrate food) has gone missing. You may find signs of vomiting (sometimes only an odor) in the bathroom (or even in bags under the bed). If your teen admits that he's vomited, he may blame it on nausea or illness. If you suspect purging, you must increase your supervision around bathroom and shower use. Specific strategies for monitoring and preventing purging are discussed in chapter 4.

Restrictive eaters may use "slimming teas," which are disguised laxatives and diuretics. You may find empty laxative packages in the trash. Teens also may engage in "cleanses," which promote extreme behaviors and thoughts, and are medically inadvisable.

Body Image Concerns

This hallmark of an adult eating disorder may not be present in children and teens. When it is present, teens may say that they feel fat, express fears about being fat, obsess about muscles, worry about a particular body part, and so on. You may observe associated behaviors in your teen, such as frequent weighing or *body checking* (looking at or pinching certain body parts to gauge size changes). She may display anxiety about getting dressed. She may exhibit body avoidance by insisting on wearing weather-inappropriate clothing (for example, a heavy hoodie in the summertime). Teens with body image obsessions may compare themselves to models or peers on social media. They may read diet tips. They may even visit pro–eating disorder websites that glorify eating disorders and advocate eating disorder behaviors (such as excessive exercising; bingeing; purging; calorie counting; fasting; using diet pills, laxatives, slimming teas, and diuretics; doing cleanses; and engaging in other ways to avoid eating or to burn more calories). Those with a stronger masculine gender identity may exhibit a focus instead on muscularity or size—characteristic of muscle dysmorphia.

A Change in Eating Behaviors

You may notice that your child's eating behaviors look different. She may be eating more slowly; drawing out meals; picking apart her sandwich to eat only the protein; blotting oil from food; eating foods in a ritualistic order; taking very small bites; cutting food into tiny pieces and pushing it around the plate; chewing excessively; or hiding food. Your teen may repeatedly heat or chill her food to keep it at the perfect temperature. She may use excessive amounts of condiments or make unusual food combinations. These behaviors and rituals may reduce anxiety—and if they are mentioned or interrupted, the teen may respond with unexpected anger or anxiety.

Loss of Menstrual Period

Cessation of a menstrual period is a significant symptom of potential eating problems. A younger teen may experience a delayed start of her first period as a result of an eating disorder. *Amenorrhea*, a condition describing previously menstruating females who have not had a period for three or more months, occurs most commonly when the body is in a state of "relative energy insufficiency," in which calorie intake is inadequate relative to energy burned. This disrupts the hormone cycle that regulates menses. Some girls with anorexia, however, continue to menstruate throughout their illness. Some stop menstruating before they start losing weight. Binge eating can also cause menstrual irregularities through metabolic or hormonal disruption (Ålgars et al. 2014).

Note that many medical professionals may ascribe menstrual irregularities to "normal" variation or athletic activity. Accepting this explanation may create another missed opportunity for diagnosis and intervention.

Other Symptoms

According to a survey of 342 parents of teens with eating disorders by the Victorian Centre of Excellence in Eating Disorders (2016), other early-warning signs parents noticed prior to their child's diagnosis included anxiety and panic attacks, changes in sleep patterns, social withdrawal, mood swings, depression, angry outbursts, irritability, and physical symptoms (such as dizziness or stomach pain).

Should I Trust My Gut?

Don't be deterred if your teenager denies a problem when confronted with your worries. Eating disorders are secretive, shameful illnesses. Have you tried to intervene during a meal and had poor results? Has your teen become upset or angry, blamed you, refused to eat altogether, or stormed away? This may have convinced you that you shouldn't intervene further. I urge you to persist! Keep trusting your parental gut. Do not let your child waste away or continue to overexercise, binge, or purge.

Many parents describe the descent into an eating disorder as falling off a cliff. Usually there are subtle signs that you might not even notice or pay much attention to. Over a brief or extended period, symptoms escalate and then accelerate. Suddenly, the teen seems to have slid off the cliff into a full-blown eating disorder. At this point, it is harder work to retrieve the teen. You and a professional team will need rappelling equipment to rescue him from the ravine.

How Do Eating Disorders Work?

Dietary restriction—simply put, eating too little to maintain an optimal weight—is a central mechanism of all eating disorders. It affects the brain, fuels the binge (and purge) cycles characteristic of binge eating disorder and bulimia, and further encourages restriction in the case of anorexia nervosa. Sometimes even slight or subtle restriction may warp mood, thinking, eating patterns, and behaviors.

What Dietary Restriction Does to the Brain

The Ancel Keys Minnesota Starvation Study (Keys et al. 1950) demonstrated that many eating disorder symptoms may result from malnutrition. In this study, thirty-six men between the ages of twenty and thirty-three were screened as healthy on medical and psychological tests. They were then placed on a six-month diet, during which their usual daily intake was cut in half (to 1,570 calories). During this phase, the previously healthy men exhibited symptoms that included reduced interest in activities, depression, anxiety, irritability, and food obsessions. They were possessive and defensive about food. They displayed eating rituals. In other words, they appeared much like individuals with restrictive eating disorders. These psychologically and physically healthy men, once "starved," were no longer healthy.

Let's pause on this. The attitudes and behaviors found among patients with eating disorders (such as preoccupation with and anxiety around food) have often been considered the *causes* of an eating disorder. The Keys study suggests they may be the *symptoms*. In other words, your teen's obsessive thinking, fear of food, and problematic eating behaviors are likely the *result* of the eating disorder, not the cause. This is a radical rethinking of the situation. It suggests that the treatment models of the past, which put the burden of change on patients (rather than leveraging parents) and required a teen's motivation to engage in recovery efforts failed to account for these biological factors.

The Binge Cycle

Now let's understand the role of dietary restriction in the binge cycle. When the body consumes insufficient food, it usually primes itself for bingeing. *Binge eating*—the rapid ingestion of a large amount of food, usually accompanied by a felt loss of control—is a powerfully driven natural biological response to not having enough food.

Our bodies evolved in a food-scarce environment. To survive, our primitive ancestors had to prioritize eating above other activities. When the food supply was less secure, humans had to stock up when food *was* available. This behavior ensured their survival.

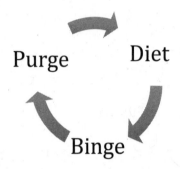

Despite what diet companies would have us believe, our bodies are not designed to diet. Our bodies haven't evolved to know that, in today's world, a lapse in eating is not a dangerous famine. So in our food-rich environment, dieting is a setup for binge eating. When a binge happens, individuals then resolve to diet or restrict again, attempting even more control over their shape, weight, and eating. Some may purge to try to minimize the effects of the binge. Either way, more dieting follows, and the cycle repeats.

Negative Energy Balance

Among mental disorders, eating disorders are unique because they disrupt eating. This creates a *negative energy balance*, a state in which a person burns more energy through physical activity than is consumed through food.

This negative energy balance seems to have specific effects on the brains of those who develop anorexia nervosa. For most people, a negative energy balance is unpleasant. They may become irritable or fatigued, or have trouble concentrating. However, for many who are prone to develop anorexia nervosa, the negative energy balance is pleasant. They experience a calming effect when they overexercise or eat insufficiently, which may then encourage more restriction or exercise. Thus, a negative energy balance can be a trap for people with anorexia (Kaye et al. 2013). Researchers do not know why restriction has such different outcomes—anorexia for some, binge eating for others.

The common essential—although not sufficient—element for recovery from all these disorders is *regular eating*: distinct meals and snacks at regular intervals throughout the day. Regular eating involves consuming appropriate volumes of food that will sustain a healthy weight. Regular eating is critical for breaking a binge or purge cycle, for reversing a negative energy balance, for weight gain, and for restoring optimal brain function. Thus, regardless of the particular form your child's eating disorder takes, the path to recovery looks much the same. This is where you can help the most.

What Does It Feel Like to Have an Eating Disorder?

Parents often ask me to talk to their teen about the eating disorder and the urgency of eating more, with the hope that their usually rational child will bend to my expert advice. Parents want their teen to return home after an appointment and eat normal amounts without putting up a fuss. This rarely happens. Understanding the mindset that sustains an eating disorder—and what it feels like to have the disorder—will help explain.

Illogical thinking. People with eating disorders commonly hold powerful beliefs about food and weight that appear irrational to others. They have thoughts such as: "I'm fat," "Any amount of dessert will cause me immediately to gain weight," "White flour is poisonous," and so on. You may be tempted to reason with your teen, but I have never seen this tactic work. This can be a frustrating part of the illness. A teen who is smart, logical, and rational in most areas of his life may become completely unreasonable when it comes to the topics of food and weight.

An unwelcome voice. In her book *Life Without Ed: How One Woman Declared Independence from Her Eating Disorder and How You Can Too*, Jenni Schaefer characterizes her eating disorder thoughts as an internal dialogue with an abusive boyfriend named "Ed." Many eating disorder sufferers report intrusive thoughts—even "voices" in their own head—that say things like, "You're fat." "You don't deserve to eat this." "You're worthless." Most people find it hard to eat appropriately when the eating disorder is running interference (Schaefer and Rutledge 2004).

Shame. Many people with eating disorders, especially those who binge or purge, feel extreme shame about these behaviors. They may hide the behaviors or lie to conceal their actions. This is one reason it can be so difficult for parents to recognize eating disorder behaviors. But the shame also explains the challenges of addressing the disorder head-on. I suggest some strategies for reducing shame in chapter 4.

Anxiety. Most teens with eating disorders face extreme anxiety every time they eat. For them, each meal can feel like being asked to jump out of an airplane. They will do almost anything they can to avoid that anxiety, including lying, hiding food, purging, or becoming violent or threatening to themselves or others. When parents understand how much fear and anxiety accompany the act of eating, it is easier to understand why teens with eating disorders behave as they do. This doesn't mean that you shouldn't push your child to eat—rather, you should do so with great compassion.

Inability to see the need for help. The word "anosognosia" may be hard to pronounce, but all you need remember is what it means: the inability to recognize that one is ill. It's not conscious denial; it's a brain condition. Anosognosia has been identified in eating disorders and occurs in individuals with schizophrenia or brain damage. Patients with anosognosia neither believe there's anything wrong with them nor perceive the severity of their illness. When your teen is suffering from a potentially fatal mental illness and refuses treatment because she does not believe there is a problem, the risks increase. She may be incapable of the traditional insight-oriented eating disorder therapy, which focuses on getting the person to understand the problem in order to solve it. This explains why treatments such as FBT, grounded in parent involvement, may be more successful: when the parents do the heavy lifting to ensure adequate food intake, weight gain, and interruption of eating disorder behaviors, it doesn't matter if the teen thinks that she is sick.

ONLINE ACTIVITY 1: My Teen's Eating, Exercise, and Body Image Symptoms

If you would like to assess the symptoms you observe in your child, please download this survey at http://www.newharbinger.com /40439. Identifying your child's behavior will help you to pinpoint areas of concern. This will later help you to determine issues on which to focus and set goals. In future chapters, you'll learn strategies to address the problem areas you note on the survey.

Closing Thoughts

In this chapter we have explored different types and features of eating disorders and how they impact your teen. This information sets the foundation for understanding how to help your child recover.

CHAPTER 2

Putting Parents in Charge

Now that you know how eating disorders may be affecting your teen, it's time to understand the important role you can play in helping her recover. In this chapter you will learn more about family-based treatment (FBT), a parent-involved eating disorder therapy that provides the foundation for the strategies in this book.

A Brief History of Treatment for Eating Disorders

The exclusion of families from the treatment of their child's eating disorders dates back to at least the late 1800s. The English physician Sir William Gull, one of the first to write about anorexia nervosa, suggested that "relations and friends" were "generally the worst attendants" for patients with the disease (Gull 1873, 501). This bias set the tone for many years. Patients were removed from their families and sent away to treatment facilities.

In the 1960s, family therapist Salvador Minuchin redefined anorexia nervosa as the result of problematic family interactions and proposed structural family therapy to treat the disorder. This treatment model had the goal of changing family interactions to cure the eating disorder. Viewing parents as part of the solution represented some progress, but families were still viewed as causing the illness. Parents were not empowered so much as they were targets of treatment.

In the 1970s, psychoanalyst Hilde Bruch proposed that anorexia nervosa had at its core "excessive closeness and overintense involvements" in the family (Bruch 1978, 106), which caused patients to fail to develop appropriate autonomy. Consequently, she advocated for individual therapy to help patients "develop a valid self-concept and the capacity for self-directed action." (Bruch 1978, 123)

Many therapists practice various forms of psychoanalytic or psychodynamic therapies. This treatment typically views an eating disorder as an expression of a deeper internal conflict, the result of a trauma, or a response to an earlier relationship issue. This type of therapy has traditionally focused on trying to develop insight into the underlying causes in order to overcome symptoms.

Today, these ideas and older models persist. There remain many providers who focus treatment on helping teens individuate from parents, search for a presumptive underlying family cause, or prescribe sending teens away to a residential facility. For some children, residential treatment may be necessary, but this approach can come with risks. Parents are still often told to back off and specifically avoid managing their child's eating behaviors.

Such treatments are out of date. We know that families do not cause eating disorders. Parents with teens who refuse to eat may appear upset and overinvolved, but this may be a symptom of the crisis rather than the cause. Any family wrestling with a life-threatening, out-of-control, and confusing problem will naturally look anxious and stressed. This is often a healthier response than neglecting the issue and letting it persist. I believe the misguided treatments of the past have contributed to the long length of illness and poorer treatment outcomes often associated with eating disorders.

Unfortunately, some treatment professionals persist in the outdated idea that parents cause eating disorders. Don't believe it. Parents do not cause eating disorders. This misplaced guilt can be debilitating. When a professional disempowers you, or you back away while your teen struggles with a mental health problem, your teen's recovery is handicapped.

Eating Disorder Treatment Settings in the United States

Levels of care for eating disorders in the United States have a distinct hierarchy (Anderson et al. 2017). From most to least intensive, the levels are as follows:

Medical hospitalization is twenty-four-hour care in a medical hospital, typically required for patients who are not medically stable and need round-the-clock medical monitoring. Care can include intravenous fluids, tube feeds, and constant monitoring of vital signs.

A residential treatment center (RTC) provides twenty-four-hour care for those who are medically stable but require round-the-clock supervision of behaviors and meals. Patients attend group therapy and sessions with a psychiatrist, therapist, and dietitian.

A partial hospitalization program (PHP) allows the patient to sleep at home and attend a treatment center during the day. Individuals can attend the program a minimum of five days a week for times usually ranging from six to eleven hours per day. Most meals are taken at the treatment center, but the patient has some meals at home. Patients attend group and individual sessions as they do in an RTC.

Intensive outpatient treatment (IOP) usually includes three hours of programming for two to three days a week. The patient lives at home and is often able to work or attend school. Treatment usually includes one meal or snack per visit.

Outpatient treatment usually consists of individual meetings once or twice a week with a therapist, dietitian, or both.

Food: The Right Medicine

Psychotherapy alone is usually inadequate to treat a teen eating disorder. Many teens with eating disorders are unwilling to engage in therapy, and, even when they do, they do not have the same capacity for insight as adults.

Eating disorders seem less responsive to psychiatric medications than other mental health disorders (Flament, Bissada, and Spettigue 2012). No medication has demonstrated consistent success in clinical trials for anorexia nervosa (Walsh, Yager, and Solomon 2013). (Medications may help for co-occurring issues such as anxiety or depression, once your teen's nutrition and eating patterns have returned to optimal levels.)

So, if individual talk therapy is not an effective treatment for teens with eating disorders, what is?

The fact is, eating disorders are, in large part, a biological issue (Keys at al. 1950). Your teen with an eating disorder is sick and needs medicine to heal. That medicine is *food*. By *food* I do not mean specific nutrients; rather, I mean the development of healthy eating habits that include regular balanced meals in adequate amounts. This applies to a teen with any eating disorder, not just anorexia nervosa. In most cases, an eating disorder will prevent a teen from making healthy decisions on his own. Think of your teen as functioning like a much younger child when it comes to food. Your primary job is to take charge and help your teen take his medicine. Your goal is to restore your teen to optimal brain and body health so he may flourish and become an independent adult.

Family-Based Treatment: A New Approach Involving Parents

FBT for teen anorexia nervosa originated at the Maudsley Hospital in London, England, in the late 1970s and early 1980s by two family therapists, Christopher Dare and Ivan Eisler. In 1994, Daniel Le Grange brought the treatment to Stanford University, where he teamed up with James Lock, and then to the University of Chicago in 1998. Together they published the first U.S. treatment manual in 2001 (Lock et al. 2001). Shortly thereafter, they began conducting clinical trials of the manualized treatment at Stanford and Chicago. Treatment trials have continued at these and other sites in the United States and abroad. In some places the method (and name) differs slightly from the one in the FBT manual—for instance, in the UK, similar approaches are referred to as *anorexia nervosa–focused family therapy for children and young people* (FT-AN) or the equivalent for bulimia: FT-BN.

The treatment has been successfully adapted for teenagers with bulimia nervosa and young adults with eating disorders. To date, several studies have shown that teens who receive FBT recover faster and at a higher rate than teens who receive traditional individual therapy (Lock et al. 2010; Le Grange et al. 2007). FBT results in psychological recovery for the teen as well as improved family communication and decreased family conflict. Accordingly, practice guidelines for the treatment of eating disorders prescribe that parents be routinely included in the treatment of teens (Yager et al. 2012).

Two elements of FBT that have revolutionized the treatment landscape are:

1. Making the family the center of the treatment team

2. Prioritization of full nutrition and cessation of eating disorder behaviors

Let's talk about each of these in turn.

Family Is Central

FBT respects the power of family bonds, empowering parents to use their love to help their teen. Caring for an ill teen in your home and nurturing her back to health is an act of love. FBT allows your teen to remain at home with you, surrounded by caring family members who are helping to fight off the eating disorder. The entire family (including siblings) usually attends every treatment session. You are not an obstacle but a crucial partner in recovery. What a difference!

FBT is often confused with traditional "family therapy," which is frequently employed in the treatment of eating disorders and explores family functioning to address the teen's eating disorder. However, traditional family therapy does not prioritize feeding or address symptoms as

FBT does. While FBT uses some traditional family therapy techniques, it differs in that it is a behavior-focused approach.

FBT treatment prioritizes helping a teen with an eating disorder return to optimal brain functioning, to reach a healthy weight if weight gain is needed, and to stop binge eating or purging. Because eating disorders have a high mortality rate, as well as potential for other serious medical issues, parents are coached to treat an eating disorder as seriously as they would cancer and to make supervision of every meal a priority—even going so far as eating meals with the teen at school.

Addressing the Symptoms

FBT focuses on achieving recovery by treating the symptoms directly. Some parents and even some treatment providers worry that this approach is superficial and ignores the underlying issues. I can understand this. Focusing on food, regular eating, and regulation of weight and health may seem mundane.

But it works!

There is no evidence that an underlying issue—if one even exists— must be addressed in order to cure an eating disorder. This is especially true for teens with illnesses of relatively short duration. As discussed in the previous chapter, many of the "underlying issues" that people identify with eating disorders (preoccupation with and anxiety around food, a desire to control one's eating, or a negative body image) are actually *symptoms* of the disorder. Research shows that the negative energy balance, delayed meals, or weight loss indicative of an eating disorder need not even arise from an intentional desire to diet or restrict food. In many cases, eating disorders emerged after patients lost weight unintentionally for unrelated reasons such as wisdom tooth extraction, pneumonia, mononucleosis, or an increase in sports training (Brandenburg and Andersen 2007). Only after the energy imbalance or weight loss occurred did the teen fixate on further dieting.

My colleague Tabitha Farrar, a recovered patient and eating disorder recovery coach, proposes an analogy: when a patient presents with lung cancer, which do we address first—the reasons he or she started smoking or the cancer itself?

Similarly, when a person with an eating disorder has food obsessions, restricted eating patterns, episodes of bingeing or purging, or dangerously low weight, should we treat these symptoms before examining why he or she lost weight, started a diet, or started bingeing or purging? Emphatically *yes!* A return to healthier eating behaviors and stabilization of weight often relieves many of these eating disorder symptoms.

Although the process of helping your teen normalize her eating and weight may increase symptoms of depression and anxiety in the short term, it is prudent to first return your teen to her optimal nutrition and then see which (if any) issues remain.

After your teen has resumed regular eating and has adequate nutrition for higher-level brain functioning, individual psychotherapy may be added to support the cognitive, emotional, and attitude changes necessary for continued freedom from the eating disorder. If your child is older or has other problems that do not resolve with a return to optimal nutrition, she may benefit from supplementary psychotherapy. Learning to manage anxiety or traits that may have contributed to the disorder, such as perfectionism, should come after the return of physical and cognitive health. Issues can be addressed in their appropriate sequence. Along the way you may avoid spending money on unnecessary services and treatment.

What Parent-Supported Recovery May Look Like

Below are two accounts from parents who supported their teens in recovery using the tactics I will be teaching you. First we will hear from the father of Gemma, who was twelve when diagnosed with anorexia nervosa. Initially, her family did not play an active role in her treatment. Later, they learned about FBT and took a more directive role.

> It took four months and many doctor visits to get a diagnosis of
> anorexia nervosa. By this time, Gemma had become medically
> unstable and had spent five weeks in the hospital for medical
> monitoring. After discharge in April 2014, treatment focused on

Gemma needing to choose to recover, and she was put in charge of her own meals and snacks. Progress was painfully slow. Although she was clearly still unwell, she was deemed "recovered" in September 2014.

In January 2015, we arranged a meeting with a psychologist because Gemma was losing weight rapidly. We proposed strategies to help Gemma, but the psychologist rejected our offers. The psychologist said Gemma should continue to control meals without our input. She believed our daughter should be allowed to choose her portion sizes, leave portions of the meal unfinished, and even not eat if she didn't wish to. She thought it was okay for Gemma to go to school even though she was weak and unable to concentrate.

The psychologist believed our child was healthy and recovered from anorexia nervosa. We were viewed as overbearing and controlling parents. Our clearly unwell thirteen-year-old daughter was left responsible for her own recovery, and the psychologist's opinion was that we were part of her problem.

To turn things around for our daughter we had to do something different. We felt the treatment was pulling our family apart. Gemma needed help—our help! So we took full control of all meals. We no longer allowed her to measure her food. Most important, we needed her to trust in us to help her get well again. After searching the Internet for advice, we found and adapted FBT in a way that worked for us—but without a supporting therapist.

We assumed full responsibility for Gemma's path to recovery. After sixteen wasted months of "treatment" that had allowed anorexia to thrive, within the space of only four months we got Gemma to a weight that was appropriate for her natural growth charts.

I then found EDPS [Eating Disorder Parent Support], an excellent parent support group, and the F.E.A.S.T. [Families Empowered and Supporting the Treatment of Eating Disorders]. Around the Dinner Table forum. Both were invaluable in reaffirming our beliefs. As Gemma's body and mind healed, she recognized how much healthier she was feeling. Over the past eighteen months there have been occasional blips that are teaching her how to recognize the signs of relapse. Gemma is far more aware of her illness now and of what she needs to do to maintain her recovery as she grows older. She feels safe knowing that we are here to guide and help along the way whenever needed. Gemma fully appreciates that she would not have been able to get better without our support.

Now let's hear about Taylor, who was diagnosed with anorexia nervosa at the age of ten. Her mother learned about FBT early in her illness and started applying the strategies from the outset.

Taylor was diagnosed in May 2011, at the age of ten. I recognized something was amiss months before her official diagnosis. In the five months prior, we visited our family doctor four times. I raised the spectre of an eating disorder (ED), but despite ongoing unexplained weight loss, I was reassured that "all was fine." By May 2011, Taylor's eating had become truly problematic, and so, not knowing what else to do, I took to the Internet. By sheer luck, I found links to F.E.A.S.T. and spent an entire weekend reading about FBT and the biological underpinnings of eating disorders. I had read that early and aggressive treatment was necessary, and I awoke on Monday morning with a plan to refeed my daughter. I kept Taylor home from school and sat at the dinner table gently encouraging her to eat. The more I tried the less she ate—I knew I needed help. Over the course of two weeks she stopped eating completely and was admitted to the specialized pediatric ED unit. She was discharged some eight weeks later, medically stable but still below her proper weight, and still very ill.

We immediately began an outpatient FBT program. Caring for a child with an eating disorder is daunting, disorienting, all-encompassing, and isolating. Our home became a miniature eating disorder treatment unit. To say I relied heavily on peer support and our FBT team is an understatement. I was encouraged by both to take control of all meals and snacks (six a day), and I aimed for a gain of two pounds per week. I adjusted and closed loopholes until I achieved it.

Every week—then biweekly, then monthly—what I was doing at home was reinforced in FBT sessions. I would discuss the week's progress, and we would troubleshoot as partners. I was encouraged to educate myself and voice my views and opinions. I was heard and my thoughts were respected. This was profound. It allowed me to regain my confidence as a parent and trust my instinct, which in turn made me a much stronger caregiver. My instinct told me to push my daughter's weight up past the number our team had set, and this helped us manage well though the high-growth puberty years. My instinct told me to ask for a nasogastric tube backup plan, which allowed us to be able to counter full refusal. My instinct told me to tackle Taylor's rigid clothing restriction much as we had addressed food, and though this was unorthodox, the team followed my lead.

Taylor gained twenty pounds in the hospital during her eight-week stay, another thirty at home over three months, and another twenty over the next few years. I was able to match the accomplishments in the hospital in large part because our FBT team had confidence in my ability to care for my child. Our FBT team also helped frame Taylor's perception of my role in her care. They viewed me as vital to her treatment and conveyed this in ways that allowed her to trust me and, in turn, trust the process.

We have, as a family, managed through this illness as unscathed as possible. Our experience with ED was harrowing, but it was not damaging. My daughter is now a healthy and happy sixteen-year-old, and I have a firm belief that the illness is treatable and that I can care for my daughter. I can't stress the significance of this enough. My daughter was ten at first diagnosis. Had I not been able to manage, Taylor may have spent the better part of her adolescence ill and out of her home.

These parents helped their teens with eating disorders heal and continue along the road of teen development. You can do this too.

What You Will Be Doing

In this chapter, we have discussed FBT's first major contribution to the treatment of eating disorders: the central role of parents. In the remainder of this book, we will discuss the second: helping your teen to eat adequately and stop behaviors such as bingeing, purging, and excessive exercising.

In the coming chapters you will be asked to prepare, plan, and oversee your teen's meals and provide supervision to prevent other eating disorder behaviors. Your initial goals for your child will be normalization of eating and related behaviors, which may include any or all of the following:

- Eliminating dietary restriction via regular eating

- Promoting weight gain

- Stopping the binge-purge cycle

- Stopping excessive exercise

- Increasing flexible eating

- Eliminating other associated eating disorder behaviors

You may tackle other eating disorder behaviors (such as cutting food into tiny pieces, frequent weighing, or refusal to sit) once eating is going more smoothly. A number of these behaviors may subside on their own once the major problems are addressed.

If you are starting to worry that this whole parent-involved treatment will not work for your child, you are not alone in your thinking. I've heard it all: "My teen is too old." "My child is too independent." "I'm not strong enough." "We are too busy." None of these factors has proven to be a deal-breaker for a successful execution of meal support and other strategies outlined in this book.

This Will Seem Hard at First

Research and my clinical experience show that many families can successfully help their adolescents recover using these techniques.

Recognize that when you first start taking over meals in this way, it is unlikely to go smoothly. Caring for an adolescent with an eating disorder has a steep learning curve. Although taking charge of your teen's recovery often starts tumultuously, it becomes easier with practice.

Here's how one parent describes the experience with her teenager, who has anorexia nervosa. From the first weekend of taking charge of recovery:

> Beth refused to eat breakfast and just stormed to her room. As a consequence, we are holding her back from her weekend volunteer activity at Children's Hospital. I feel bad, as it is a positive activity for the community.
>
> I am holding strong. Was able to even ignore and work through last night's outburst of "go f— yourself." All of this is so incongruent with Beth's previous behavior and overall disposition.

After about one week:

> I am amazed at the difference just a few days make. Her anger has decreased and she is beginning to manage previously uncomfortable levels of food. I am gradually increasing amounts as well as beginning to include her few taboo items. Husband or I have been going to school for lunch this week. The first time she was utterly pissed—the second time, she accepted. The angry comments are still there, but a bit decreased, and even Beth has noticed that her anxiety has lessened. In one particularly rational moment, she commented that she wished that we would have done this sooner.

Getting Additional Support

You and your family are not alone in fighting an eating disorder. In fact, there are many individuals, groups, and organizations that can provide invaluable support, guidance, and information. See a list of these resources at http://www.newharbinger.com/40439.

Closing Thoughts

You now understand why your child needs your help. You have read accounts by two parents who helped their teens recover using these methods. Both parents trusted their parental instincts, learned everything they could about parent-supported eating disorder treatment, and took a firm stance against their teens' eating disorders. In the next chapter, you will chart a road map for parent-supported treatment for your teen.

CHAPTER 3

Preparing to Take Charge of Recovery

Melanie was a fourteen-year-old with anorexia nervosa who had achieved only minimal weight gain while in a treatment program. Her height appeared stunted. Her parents were frustrated with her slow weight gain and the program's reluctance to include them in her treatment. It felt unnatural for their family. They removed Melanie from the program and started administering meals at home. Shortly thereafter, they sought my guidance.

Melanie ate a restricted range of foods, primarily fruits and vegetables. In consultation with me, one of the family's first tasks was to establish a home-based eating structure to promote recovery. Concerned that she would not eat at school, her parents decided to keep her home so they could supervise all meals. Both parents traveled frequently, so they enlisted a babysitter to share meal planning and supervision. Melanie's grandmother also visited for about a month to help. All the caregivers—her parents, the babysitter, and the grandmother—had to maintain a united front with consistent messages about the importance of proper nutrition and full recovery.

I helped Melanie's family, and I will help yours as well. In this chapter, you will learn to assemble your treatment team (if you haven't already) and to align with your partner (if you have one) and other caregivers. You will receive frameworks for understanding the development of eating independence and weight gain goals as you prepare to help your teen.

Warning About Refeeding Syndrome

Before you start attempting to help your teen gain weight, I must warn you about *refeeding syndrome*. It's uncommon, but it can be fatal. Refeeding syndrome is a sudden shift in fluids and minerals caused by the rapid renourishment of a person who is in a state of starvation. During starvation, the body breaks down muscle and fat tissue, and uses them for energy. The resumption of eating reintroduces dietary glucose into the bloodstream. When cells start drawing in glucose as a source of energy, minerals are taken in as well. The sudden change in cell behavior can create a precipitous drop in bloodstream mineral concentration that impacts the functioning of vital organs. Potential consequences may include irregular heart rate, congestive heart failure, respiratory failure, coma, seizures, skeletal-muscle weakness, loss of control of body movements, and brain damage. Unfortunately, symptoms may not emerge until they are catastrophic.

Any patient with negligible food intake for more than five days is at risk of developing refeeding syndrome. We don't know yet how to predict who develops refeeding syndrome, so vigilance is vital. For this reason, your child should already be under a medical doctor's care; for those without access to specialized care, please seek guidance before proceeding.

The Academy for Eating Disorders (AED) provides guidelines and recommendations regarding refeeding syndrome. The AED states: "Consider initiating refeeding in an inpatient setting if one or more risk factors for refeeding are present. Ideally patients should be admitted to a hospital that has access to or onsite ED specialist support" (2016).

Due to the risk for refeeding syndrome and countless other potential medical issues related to eating disorders that are beyond this book's scope, teens with restrictive eating disorders or with significant malnutrition should always begin their nutritional rehabilitation under close medical supervision. This book is directed toward those who do not need hospitalization, are *not* at risk for refeeding syndrome, and have been medically cleared to begin or continue nutritional rehabilitation on an outpatient basis.

Assembling a Treatment Team

Ideally, every teen would have access to a full *treatment team*, each individual specialized in eating disorders and supportive of family involvement in treatment. At a minimum, the team would include:

- A medical doctor to identify and address any physical problems

- A therapist to guide the family in treatment

- A registered dietitian to advise parents on nutritional needs, if necessary

In some cases a treatment team would also include an individual therapist for the teen and a psychiatrist to prescribe and monitor psychiatric medications.

FBT calls only for a therapist to guide the parents and a medical doctor to monitor medical needs. Studies have found that a dietitian is unnecessary. But a dietitian who works with the parents—not individually with the teen—can provide valuable guidance. Dietitians often contribute to the assessment of eating disorders and can inform on nutritional and energy needs, help establish healthy goal weights, and evaluate the impact of malnourishment on growth and development.

If there are multiple providers, it is best when team members approach treatment with full agreement on treatment methods and goals. Alignment among all treatment providers allows for the consistent messaging and communication required to address serious symptoms (Spotts-De Lazzer and Muhlheim 2016; Murray, Griffiths, and Le Grange 2014). If your practitioners are not already encouraging you to play a role in your child's treatment, I recommend that you convey your desire to help your child directly.

Can I Do This Without a Therapist?

Parents may be able to begin restoring a teen's nutrition and eating patterns to his optimal levels without a therapist's involvement, although expert care can help with more challenging symptoms. Some parents claim that working with a therapist who opposes parent involvement may be worse than not having a therapist.

Should you do this without a therapist? I can't make that decision for you, but I advise you to seek an FBT therapist or other professional (therapist, medical doctor, or dietitian) who supports your active engagement with your teen's treatment. Additional resources in the online materials can help direct you to providers. At a minimum, a medical doctor should follow your teen due to the risk for serious medical complications.

Assembling a Support Team

Think about who will be on your *support team*. This usually includes:

- All involved parents (even those who do not cohabitate)

- All members of the treatment team

- Extended family members

- Close friends

- Babysitters

- Coworkers

Given the potential for extreme reactions when you take charge, you should have a shared game plan for handling situations. This will require the responsible adults in the family to develop a common understanding of the situation through candid conversation. It helps to read about eating disorders, the parent experience, and related issues.

You must be clear on your shared commitment to help your teen. You must also agree on basic treatment goals in conjunction with a treatment team. Simple shared goals—such as weight gain or cessation of purging behavior—will make it easier.

When there are two parents, you must agree upon specific strategies—otherwise, the eating disorder can pit you against one another and gain strength. For example, if Mom supervises most meals and requires Carlos to finish everything on his plate, Dad should know this is the procedure. If he does not, on a night when Mom is out and Dad is supervising, Carlos may convince Dad that Mom usually allows him to leave a portion of his rice uneaten on his plate. When Mom comes home and Dad reports on the unfinished dinner, Mom may worry that Carlos did not eat enough and become angry with Dad for handling the meal differently than she would have.

Eating disorders exploit such opportunities, making a united front more critical. Often one parent is stricter than the other. You must figure out how to be as consistent as possible. Even if you are at odds elsewhere, you may need to park these issues to prioritize saving your teen's life. When parents are divorced or separated there must be consistency between households. When separated parents share custody, they may consider adjusting custody arrangements to best support recovery.

Individual parents have unique strengths and weaknesses. Maybe one parent has more patience with the teen during meals, while the other leads meal planning and preparation. If there are two of you, recognize your different strengths and use them strategically.

Supervision of all meals (extending beyond mealtime if purging is an issue) can be daunting, especially for busy families. If there are two parents in your house you must discuss how this duty will be shared. One or both parents may decide to take a leave of absence from work to arrange the eating treatment environment. In some cases, it can be helpful to have more than one adult present at meals. If there is only one parent, the burden may be greater, but creative solutions are possible. Grandparents and other extended family members, as well as babysitters or other paid caregivers, can help with supervising meals—I have worked with several families who have had grandparents from other countries fly in to assist.

Systematic meal supervision can be like running a treatment center for one. Please remember that this will not last forever. The sooner you confront the eating disorder, establish a pattern of regular eating, and stop other eating disorder behaviors, the sooner your child will be on a path to recovery and health. And once you develop momentum, it gets easier.

Some teens will need round-the-clock supervision if they are impulsive, engage in secretive exercise, or are at risk for bingeing or purging (more on this in chapter 4). Although managing the disorder at home can be burdensome, many families find it preferable to sending a teen away to a residential treatment center, where others will provide this level of supervision.

The Role of Siblings

Eating disorders (and related issues) also impact siblings. A teen's eating disorder may increase pressure on other children in the family. Sibling responses vary. Some want to minimize their own needs because they see the stress their sister's problem is placing on their parents. Others may act out to compete for attention. Many siblings worry tremendously about their sister.

Explain to all your children in age-appropriate terms what is happening and that they are not to blame. You can tell them that it's important to be kind to the sister who is suffering. You may clarify that even though you seem preoccupied with the eating disorder, you understand that each child has his or her own needs. You can encourage siblings to share their own feelings about the situation. They may feel frightened for the family, sad and scared for their sister, or angry that their sister has upset the entire family. It is best to be open and honest, especially since siblings may share genes that could play a role in causing the eating disorder and be at increased risk.

Siblings can also be an asset. FBT encourages siblings to provide support and distraction during and after meals, and to continue to engage the sick sister in activities outside of meals.

One job siblings preferably should not undertake is meal support. Unless they are much older, have their own established autonomy, and have long been in a more custodial role, do not ask siblings to help supervise meals or try to get their sister to eat. This should remain the job of adults. Keeping parents in charge and the children aligned strengthens the sibling bond and prevents siblings from developing feelings of disloyalty.

ONLINE ACTIVITY 2: Who Is on My Team?

To help you determine who you'd like on your child's treatment and support teams and their roles, please download this handy planner from http://www.newharbinger.com/40439. It will help you organize and keep track of your allies in fighting the eating disorder.

A Road Map to Eating Independence

In my work with teens, I have developed an eating independence continuum, based on teen development, that is useful for thinking about the process of recovery.

Eating Independence Continuum

This diagram represents common steps toward eating independence. In healthy developing children, independence will progress naturally with age (though not necessarily in this *exact* order).

- Most preschoolers can handle steps 1 to 4 (eating what they are given).

- Elementary school children commonly master steps 5 to 9 (making simple choices).

- Middle schoolers usually master steps 10 to 12 (making more complex decisions about eating in varied settings).

- With the independence of driving, high schoolers progress through steps 13 and 14 (limited independent eating).

- Step 15 (independently choosing, planning, and preparing food) is usually not mastered until adulthood. In my experience, some young adults, eating disordered or not, often struggle with this step.

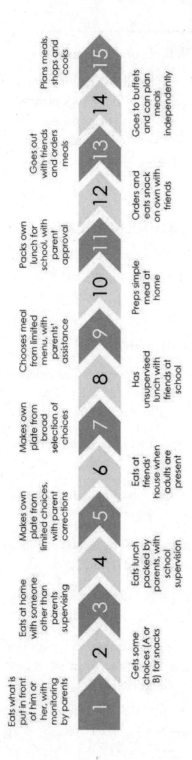

1. Eats what is put in front of him or her, with monitoring by parents

2. Gets some choices (A or B) for snacks

3. Eats at home with someone other than parents supervising

4. Eats lunch packed by parents, with school supervision

5. Makes own plate from limited choices, with parent corrections

6. Eats at friends' house when adults are present

7. Makes own plate from broad selection of choices

8. Has unsupervised lunch with friends at school

9. Chooses meal from limited menu, with parents' assistance

10. Preps simple meal at home

11. Packs own lunch for school, with parent approval

12. Orders and eats snack on own with friends

13. Goes out with friends and orders meals

14. Goes to buffets and can plan meals independently

15. Plans meals, shops and cooks

Teens with an eating disorder are often characterized as being *developmentally regressed* in their ability to eat independently in a way that appropriately nourishes their bodies. They may lag behind others their age on the eating independence continuum. As a result, parents must take charge of feeding in the same way they may have done when the teen was a much younger child.

While this may sound oppressive, please remember that you are taking charge only of your teen's meals, not other aspects of his life that do not impact eating or the eating disorder. This does not infantilize your teen; it allows him to restore his full cognitive function to resume normal teen independence as he escapes the eating disorder's grip. During the course of treatment, one goal will be to move your teen to the right of the continuum and gradually return greater control over his own eating and related behaviors.

One common misunderstanding about FBT is that it is limited to putting parents in charge of feeding. Too many parents end up thinking that this starting point is also the end goal. The calculated return of control to the teen is just as important as the parent taking charge of meals and restoring nutrition and eating patterns. Your job is unfinished until your teen can manage his eating at an age-appropriate level of independence.

We will talk more about the specific steps toward recovery and independent eating in chapter 9. However, at this time let's consider how far your child needs to go—how many steps are required to get him to full age-appropriate independent eating.

Most families start FBT with the parents fully in charge of all meals (at step 1). There may be exceptions to this. For example, teens with bulimia nervosa often seem more motivated to recover and, as a result, can be more capable of collaborating with treatment—in which case they may not need to have *all* control taken away. They may be able to participate in some meal planning, choose their own snacks, or eat lunches on their own (steps 2 through 5). Similarly, an older teen whose illness is less severe may be capable of greater participation in treatment. I have worked with some older teens who were able to start at steps 6 or 7, meaning they could make some choices around food and handle some meals in settings without parents present.

If your teenager has demonstrated that she can handle these tasks without eating disorder behaviors, you might begin further along the continuum. Some of my teen clients began with eating a home-packed lunch (step 8) independently at school with the expectation that they complete it. If they did not gain weight, parents resumed supervision of lunch. However, these are the exceptions rather than the rule.

Treatment goals should be appropriate for the age of your child. The older children are when they enter treatment, the further along the continuum your treatment goal should be. For example, young children treated for eating disorders only need to go as far as about step 8. Middle schoolers shouldn't be expected to independently plan and cook their own meals (step 15) by the end of treatment. However, an older teenager must master this step. For this reason, recovery at older ages can be a harder and longer process.

ONLINE ACTIVITY 3:
Eating Independence Scale

Not sure where to begin? Download this worksheet from http:// www.newharbinger.com/40439 to help you plan your course of action in fighting the eating disorder.

Weight Gain

If your child has been restricting his intake, he may need to gain weight as part of recovery. This is true not only for those who have anorexia nervosa but also for many with bulimia nervosa and binge eating disorder. *Weight suppression* (falling beneath a previous higher weight) is believed to be a primary driver of binge eating (Keel and Heatherton 2010). You can't have recovery from the mental symptoms of anorexia while you're below the weight nature intended for you.

Using Growth Curves

The determination of ideal body weight is complicated (Lebow, Sim, and Accurso 2017). Body weight and height are largely genetically determined. Contrary to the promises of diet companies and the ideology of the war on fat, not every individual will place neatly into the "average" weight category based on age and height.

Consider foot size, which has a normal distribution within the population. While the average woman today has an 8½ shoe size, most do not—some will have size 5 and others will have size 10. So it is with body weight. Not everyone is predestined to have a body weight in the 50th percentile—some will be heavier and some lighter.

At each of your child's well visits, your pediatrician should be documenting her growth on the CDC growth charts, which plot height, weight, and body-mass index (BMI) against age-based averages. The input should generate unique growth curves for your teen.

In healthy children and teens, height and weight each increase along a consistent growth curve. Some children and teens grow steadily along the 50th percentile, while others grow steadily along the 25th percentile and still others along the 95th percentile. For individuals, height and weight percentages may be similar or different. For some children and teens, a weight on the 60th percentile and height on the 40th percentile is normal. This defines the growth curves for that individual.

It is *falling off* the growth curve trend line for height, weight, or BMI that may indicate a problem requiring correction. Many children who develop eating disorders do not experience actual weight loss. Teens should be growing at this age—they commonly gain thirty pounds during puberty. But if a child who has always tracked along the 75th percentile for either height or weight suddenly tracks along the 50th percentile, then there is reason for curiosity and concern even if the child is not technically underweight. Sometimes young people with eating disorders fall off their height curves before they fall off their weight curves, which is why both should be tracked. And even teens who are done growing are expected to continue to gain weight, albeit more slowly, through late adolescence and into early adulthood.

Professionals also use growth curves to establish target weights for recovery. Research shows that these curves, when available, are more accurate than using population averages to determine an individual's treatment goal weight. They can help a professional to accurately estimate the weight at which females will resume menses (periods) following amenorrhea due to malnutrition (Harrison et al. 2013). (Return of menstruation is a necessary but not sufficient sign of adequate weight gain—some females resume menses at very low weights.)

If you lack access to your child's growth charts and cannot reconstruct their growth curves from other height and weight records (such as baby books), this becomes an even more imperfect science. You may still be able to develop some guidance based on old photos and the parents' and siblings' height and weight profiles.

A sample weight chart is below. As you can see, Stacy was tracking at or above the 50th percentile for weight until age nine. By age eleven, her curve had dropped below the 25th percentile. An intervention by parents at age eleven returned her to the 50th percentile by age fourteen.

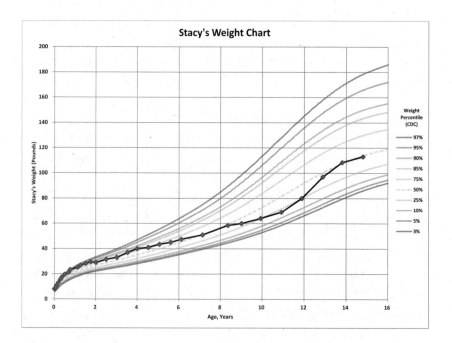

Setting Target Weights for Recovery

The men in the Minnesota Starvation Study (see chapter 1) tended to gain about 10 percent over their initial weights when they resumed eating normally (Garner 1998). And many parents of teens who had eating disorders state that their teen did not complete their brain healing until he or she reached 10 percent above the weight indicated by his or her personal growth curve. They report that their teen continued to be plagued by eating disorder thoughts until this higher weight threshold was achieved, at which point they noticed a considerably improved state, described by one parent as "coming out of a fog." Parents and clinicians have noted that sometimes a few extra pounds can make all the difference in a teen's recovery. At a higher weight, the eating disorder thoughts tend to relax and treatment becomes easier.

Parents looking back on a teen's recovery report that practitioners tend to set initial target weights too low. Even treatment providers may be susceptible to weight stigma encouraged by society's war on obesity. Consequently, they may err on the side of under-restoring a teen in recovery. They also often want to avoid facing their patient's anxiety over reaching higher weights.

Remember that an irrational fear of weight gain is often a symptom of the disorder. The anxiety over being fat is more likely to significantly improve with recovery, more regular eating patterns, and—ironically— weight gain than it is with appeasement. A teen may strive to maintain a lower weight because it distresses her less, but keep in mind that there is no weight low enough to satisfy anorexia.

ONLINE ACTIVITY 4: Height and Weight Trajectories

You can plot your child's growth curve for free online at My Growth Charts (http://www.mygrowthcharts.com). Then refer to the height and weight trajectory worksheet at http://www.newharbinger .com/40439 to help you decide whether your teen needs to gain weight. Ways to help with weight gain are addressed in chapters 5 and 6.

Parents' Weight Concerns

A common and confusing issue may be concern about your own weight. Weight stigma is commonplace, and parents tend to have their own history of dieting. If you do diet, know that you did not cause your teen's eating disorder, and you should not blame yourself. Many teens go on diets and don't develop eating disorders. Blaming yourself is a waste of time and energy that you need for your child.

However, it may be important to examine your own behaviors and decide whether they are consistent with the goals for your child's recovery. Dieting in the household could reinforce thoughts and behaviors you want to eradicate as you help your teen recover from an eating disorder. Therefore, dieting is discouraged. Even so, this does not mean that you must eat exactly the same things as your teen.

Issues around your own weight can be a difficult minefield to navigate. If you tend to be on the larger side (or have been in the past), your teen may use that against you. He may attack your weight or argue that his eating disorder behaviors are no different than your dieting or exercise behaviors. When an eating disorder is active, your teen can push your buttons. Regardless of parental weight and dieting history, it is important to put that aside and focus on the health of your teen.

How One Mother Managed Her Own Weight Concerns

Read about a parent who had to face her own weight issues while caring for a teen with an eating disorder. Visit http://www.newhar binger.com/40439.

Get Ready: Be Courageous, Resourceful, Strong, and Loving

For parents this work is challenging. Many have told me this is the most difficult thing they have ever done as parents. It can feel unnatural and intrusive to supervise a teen who has been eating independently for many years. When parents get a negative reaction like those I describe in the next chapter, they worry that they are "doing it wrong" or harming their teenager. No, not at all! Remember: you are saving your child's life. Many families become even closer after having battled the eating disorder together.

There is no way around this, only through. Just as your teen will have to learn to tolerate his distress and anxiety—skills we will discuss in later chapters—you will have to do the same.

Let's return to Melanie, the teen described at the beginning of this chapter. Melanie's parents established a strict structure and supervised her eating at regular intervals throughout the day. She initially reacted to meals with anxiety and anger. Over time, she became less upset during mealtimes and more flexible in her eating.

Her desire to return to school motivated her to comply with meals. Her parents developed a meal schedule that allowed her to return to school but still have supervision: she attended school for only half the day, returning home for lunch.

After three months, Melanie returned to school full-time, with decreased anxiety and depression. During the initial eight months, Melanie gained twenty-one pounds and grew a half inch. She could eat home-packed lunches on her own at school and could eat some limited foods with friends when her parents were not present. However, she still required supervision for most meals and was not ready for independent eating. Melanie still had eating disorder urges to restrict, along with guilt after eating. However, her flexibility had gradually improved. Within a year after treatment initiation, she had conquered most of her fear foods and had maintained a healthy weight (based on historical growth curves) for many months.

Closing Thoughts

In this chapter you have learned how to align your team and about the risk of refeeding syndrome. You have received frameworks for understanding the progression of eating independence and the determination of weight goals. You now are ready to start intervening on your teen's behalf!

CHAPTER 4

Strategies to Structure Recovery and Manage Behaviors

When a family begins to help a teen with an eating disorder, there are usually many issues on which to focus. In this chapter, you'll learn specific strategies to address various problems and symptoms. I will help you develop a safety plan, establish priorities, and prepare to help your teen in specific ways.

Let's begin by meeting Jasmine, a sixteen-year-old who thinks she's fat. During the past year, she has become a vegetarian, eaten restrictively, and lost approximately ten pounds. She is overexercising, bingeing, and purging in the evenings. Friends have alerted the school counselor that she throws away her lunch. She is having conflicts with friends. When her parents said they were going to supervise her eating and take charge of her recovery, she became angry and defiant and threatened to hurt herself.

If Jasmine were your teen, how would you prioritize and address these various issues?

Safety First!

When choosing the order in which to address your teen's eating disorder and related behaviors, life-threatening issues must be addressed first. The eating disorder is itself ultimately life threatening, but more imminently dangerous behaviors may arise as you treat the disorder, particularly in response to meals and other challenges. These may include running away, suicide threats, violence toward others, cutting, and other forms of self-harm.

Be Prepared for Extreme Behaviors

When you start to challenge an eating disorder, things may escalate. Even if your teen has never exhibited such behavior before, be prepared. What follows are examples of teens who displayed extreme behaviors during eating disorder recovery and how their parents managed the behaviors.

Violence

During meals, my daughter would scream and throw food. Her behavior escalated in this way before every single meal. She had never behaved in this way until we started to require her to eat. Once, she even ran away. She assaulted us and once threatened us with a knife. We would call the police. Usually she would back down before they even dispatched.

My eleven-year-old was violent toward me several times. In the most severe case he threw things at me and hit me. I de-escalated the situation by walking away and staying in a separate space until he calmed down. I did not want to add layers of guilt on top of struggling with an eating disorder, so I tried to always remember that the behaviors were part of the eating disorder and not my son's true self.

My daughter would throw plates and silverware. During meals, we did paper and plastic everything. We cooked double the necessary amount of food, as we knew most would be thrown onto the walls

and floor. As soon as she started throwing food, we would remove anything that she could throw and be within arm's reach of her. At times we had to physically restrain her from throwing chairs or running for something like a knife or a vase.

Self-Harm

After completing a meal that included feared foods, our son ran out on the balcony yelling at the top of his lungs that he wanted to die. We stayed with him and provided constant supervision.

She slept in my bedroom for months. We had alarms on doors and windows, and she was always supervised. We looked at all objects with new eyes: Can this be used to hurt? We removed all sharp items, medicines, porcelain, and glass from the house. At some point, we removed doors from doorframes. Whenever she made a suicidal threat she went to the emergency room to get evaluated. She hated it.

Running Away

Our son frequently ran away during meals. I would call the police to search for him and return him home. He learned that he would either eat or be taken by the police to a hospital.

My daughter frequently ran away to her friends' houses. In addition to using smartphone-tracking software, I worked with the local police and the parents of her friends so that everyone responded in the same way when she showed up—by letting us know where she was and returning her home.

Please remember that it is the eating disorder that makes teens do these extreme things. They are not deliberately trying to be opposi-tional or devious. An eating disorder possesses good, obedient teens to do things they wouldn't normally do. It intensifies the behavior of teens who are already stubborn or oppositional. In effect, these teens are complying with the demands of the eating disorder. They may remain compliant in other areas of their life, but they are so fearful of food and weight that they will do almost anything they can to avoid eating foods that scare them.

Have a Plan

When teens with eating disorders threaten to harm you or themselves to keep you from making them eat, their threats must be taken seriously. Even if these behaviors are just gambits, you should call their bluff. I suggest you take any threats or self-harm behavior literally and handle them as you would handle a truly suicidal teen: take him or her for a psychiatric evaluation or call the police or emergency department.

It is important to not back down and say, "Okay, never mind, you don't really need to eat that pizza" when your teen threatens you, or becomes violent, or even threatens suicide. Remember that food is also a requirement—it is in fact the medicine. Have a plan in place in case behaviors escalate. Your safety plan may include any or all of the following:

- Round-the-clock supervision (psychiatric hospitals have "watchers" assigned to monitor patients at risk for suicide)

- Sleeping in the same room as your teen

- Removing door locks or even doors

- Walking away from an aggressive child

- Physically restraining your child for a short time to keep him or her safe

- Removing sharp items, such as knives and scissors, from the house or keeping them locked up

- Locking up medications

- Calling the police

- Taking your teen to the emergency room

- Psychiatric hospitalization

Your primary goal, as always, is to keep your teen safe. You must do this by any means necessary.

During early eating disorder recovery, some teens who display repeated dangerous behaviors in response to the anxiety of eating recovery foods may not be safely manageable at home. They may require the support, structure, and containment of a higher level of treatment provided by professionals.

After addressing safety behaviors, the next symptoms to address are those core to the eating disorder, including dieting, bingeing, purging, and excessive exercise. In the next section we will discuss strategies for establishing regular eating, promoting weight gain, stopping the binge and purge cycle, preventing purges, limiting exercise, increasing food variety, and limiting access to the scale. We will briefly touch on other eating disorder behaviors.

Establishing Regular Eating

Regular eating is the centerpiece of treatment for any eating disorder. Most people with eating disorders eat irregularly and insufficiently at meals. In addition to restricting the range of foods they eat, teens may delay eating, skip meals, or consume small amounts.

Regular eating usually comprises three meals and two to three snacks evenly distributed throughout the day such as:

Breakfast (within an hour of waking)

Mid-morning snack (if breakfast and lunch are more than three hours apart)

Lunch

Afternoon snack

Dinner

Evening snack (one to two hours before going to sleep)

These should be discrete meals and snacks, not nibbling throughout the day. They must deliver food adequate to sustain a teen who might be growing or malnourished. Regular eating is equally important for teens who restrict and those who binge or purge. Research shows that over time restraint can break down, and many people with restrictive eating disorders cross over into bulimic or binge eating behaviors (Eddy et al. 2008). Regular eating may discourage this progression (Zunker et al. 2011).

Promoting Weight Gain

If your child needs to gain weight, this will be a primary focus of your meal planning. There are four main ways to help someone gain weight:

- **Increase the frequency of meals.** Instead of three meals per day, encourage six.

- **Increase the portion size.** Instead of two eggs, serve three.

- **Increase caloric density.** Provide a bowl of ice cream, which has more fat and calories than a bowl of blueberries the same size.

- **Conserve energy.** Limit activity. You can limit your teen to more sedentary activities until he is in a healthier state. This may require strict supervision—some teens will exercise in secret (sometimes even in the shower or in the middle of the night). In a hospital or a residential treatment center, teens are sometimes placed on bed rest to conserve energy. You can implement this at home too.

Stopping the Binge (and Purge) Cycle

Binge behavior is often fueled by restriction and can be exacerbated by deprivation from foods pleasurable to your teenager (which often wind up on their list of forbidden foods). Regular eating—and inclusion of the foods that are both craved and feared—mitigates binge behavior. Between meals and snacks, teens who binge eat may need to be supervised to intercept binge behavior. In extreme cases or in the case of residential treatment centers, food can be locked up between meals.

The teen is often wrestling with two conflicting drives: the urge to eat and a fear of doing so. Assess when these behaviors occur. People who binge eat will often go to the kitchen in the evening when everyone is asleep or bring binge food into their bedrooms. If teens are binge eating when they return to an empty home after school, alternative plans may have to be made. Some teens would benefit from going to a friend's house after school or staying late at school on days when an adult isn't home. For teens who binge at school on food they can buy or obtain from others, you may need to arrange for supervision during breaks or lunch. If they binge at night after everyone has gone to sleep, consider other strategies, such as reviewing sleep arrangements and restricting access to the kitchen.

One family I worked with identified their entire kitchen as a trigger. To prevent her teen from unsupervised entry into the kitchen, the mother would leave a snack of nuts with fruit on the living room table, where her daughter would eat when she arrived home from school.

Preventing Purges

Self-induced vomiting is a dangerous behavior that can lead to horrible consequences. Recurrent purging can result in a loss of electrolytes that can cause a fatal cardiac arrhythmia. Purging over extended periods of time leads to reflux of stomach contents into the esophagus; stomach acid then damages the esophagus. Damage to gums and tooth enamel also occur in the wake of prolonged exposure to stomach acid. Purging needs to be stopped, and the sooner the better.

Teens will sometimes purge in the shower to mask the sound of vomiting and to clean and soothe themselves through the process. Another common behavior is to claim nausea and purge during or immediately after a meal. If your teen were in a residential treatment center, bathroom use immediately after meals would be prohibited, and all bathroom use would be monitored. Even if it feels intrusive, this type of purge prevention in a home setting is essential. It is only when the behaviors are prevented that the teen can learn how to tolerate the underlying distress and develop healthier coping skills. We will talk more about coping skills and distress tolerance in chapter 7.

If your teen is deliberately vomiting, you will want to interrupt the behavior. Teens value privacy, so this increased level of supervision can be met with opposition. Strategies to prevent purging may include any or all of the following:

- Requiring your teen to use the bathroom before meals (so he doesn't "have to go" right after)

- Supervising your teen for up to two hours after meals (one hour may suffice)

- Prohibiting bathroom use for one hour after meals

- Accompanying your teen to the bathroom and standing outside during use so you can hear what she is doing

- Requiring your teen to leave the bathroom door cracked open so you can hear him

- Requiring your teen to let you look in the toilet before flushing

- Requiring your teen to shower with the bathroom door open

- Requiring your teen to sing or talk while using the restroom or showering

- Taking the bathroom door off the hinges (in extreme cases)

- Searching your teen's bedroom regularly

The risk of being discovered is a common deterrent for teens. One older teen was relocated from a bedroom with a private bath to a room without one. Susan, a Maryland mother of a teen with bulimia, reports:

I accompanied Danielle for every bathroom break. I stood just outside the open door, where I could observe her partial reflection in the mirror or watch her shadow on the wall. This gave her a bit of privacy. However, I once saw her head bend down. I moved into the doorway and saw that she was trying to purge into the toilet bowl between her legs. I said, "No, stop!" That purge was prevented, and she realized that I did indeed monitor, even when out of her line of sight. I also used to go into the public bathroom stall with my daughter.

Brian, a single dad from Wisconsin, says:

Although my daughter wasn't bingeing and purging, I supervised after meals just in case. She used to hide food in her clothing and try to flush it down the toilet after meals or throw it in the trash. A whole floating piece of untouched sushi gave that trick away!

Limiting Exercise

Hopefully your teen is seeing a medical doctor who can advise whether it is safe for her to exercise. Often, exercise carries additional risks and may be completely restricted by a doctor. Your teen may have a strong urge to exercise and may be exercising secretly. Common behaviors include exercising in the middle of the night, sneaking off to bedrooms to do jumping jacks, running laps during lunch at school, exercising while watching TV, standing instead of sitting to burn more calories, insisting on a walk after dinner, and even tensing leg muscles while sitting.

It's imperative to prevent your teen from excessive—or, in some cases, any—exercise, which can make weight gain harder and strengthen the eating disorder. Some strategies employed by parents include having the teen sleep with parents, requiring open doors to the bedroom, requiring the bathroom door be open during showering, electronic movement tracking, and closer supervision.

Taunisha, a South Carolina mother of a teen with anorexia, recalls:

My daughter occasionally tried to exercise in her room. I insisted that her bedroom door stay open at all times, and I took away her yoga mat. If she were caught exercising, I would take her out of

*school for the day or more and take away her computer and
makeup, which was a big deal for her at the time.*

Dani, who lives in Florida with a teen with bulimia, says:

*We had to make sure he was getting to class on time, every time—
he was often late due to walking around campus or going up and
down the stairs. We put a video monitor in his room and made him
leave bathroom doors open to make sure he wasn't trying to exercise
when alone. We never left him at home alone.*

Increasing Food Variety

Increasing the range of foods eaten is a primary goal for patients of any
diagnosis, whether anorexia nervosa, bulimia nervosa, binge eating disorder, ARFID, or OSFED. Research shows that individuals who were
successful in recovery consume a more varied diet and more dietary fat
(Schebendach et al. 2012). Individuals who eat a restricted range of
foods can face greater risk of getting too little food in certain circum-
stances. For example, a road trip during which the only stop for meals
may be a restaurant along the interstate could be problematic for an
individual who refuses to eat any fast food or will only eat a side salad.
Reluctance to eat energy-dense foods could trigger an energy imbalance that reactivates an eating disorder. You want your teenager to live
the fullest life possible and not be hampered by the eating disorder.
Specific strategies for increasing food variety will be addressed in
chapter 8, but it is important to be aware of this treatment target at the
outset.

Limiting Access to the Scale

One additional behavior that may need to be addressed at the beginning of treatment is obsessive weighing. Teens with eating disorders
often have compulsions to weigh themselves frequently and will go to
great lengths to find a scale. This behavior should be prevented. Parents
often need to hide or throw out the scale. Wendy, a mother in California,

says, "I threw away the scale and asked relatives to hide theirs if we visited. My daughter was only weighed at treatment appointments."

Handling Other Eating Behaviors

Teens may exhibit a myriad of other problematic behaviors related to both eating and the eating disorder. These may well be issues to address, but they can be handled later, after the bingeing and purging cycles have abated or weight is higher. Here are things to look for that you may want to treat later:

Mealtime behaviors

- Eating foods in a ritualistic order

- Preventing foods from touching

- Dismantling foods (for example, tearing apart a sandwich to eat only the lunch meat)

- Eating very slowly or very quickly

- Smearing food

- Chewing incessantly

- Taking tiny bites

- Hiding food

Non-mealtime behaviors

- Reading food labels

- Following social media sites that glorify thinness or eating disorder behaviors

- Engaging in obsessive size comparison with peers

- Body checking, or repeated checking of body size or body parts

- Dressing inappropriately, such as wearing overly baggy clothes, wearing long sleeves and hoodies in ninety-degree weather, or wearing light clothing in winter

- Checking behaviors or rituals that may be symptomatic of other disorders, such as OCD

ONLINE ACTIVITY 5:
Treatment Goals for My Teen

To help you determine the specific goals of your child's treatment plan, please download this handy checklist from http://www .newharbinger.com/40439. It can help you to remain focused on your key treatment objectives.

Externalize the Eating Disorder

One technique many parents find helpful is to externalize the eating disorder. This strategy is a central element of FBT and involves separating the teen from her eating disorder thoughts and behaviors. It was popularized by Jenni Schaefer in her book *Life Without Ed*, in which she characterized her eating disorder as an abusive boyfriend (Schaefer and Rutledge 2004).

I often take the metaphor in a slightly different direction, painting the picture of an external force that has invaded the teen and hijacked her brain. It can be helpful to assign a name to the illness: "the monster," "the alien," "Voldemort," or any villain that captures the teen's imagination. We can then think of the eating disorder as an intruder that needs to be vanquished. To many family members—and even to the teenager herself—the teen does seem to become a "different person" under the influence of the eating disorder, so externalizing the illness feels natural. The externalization reframes the situation: we do not say that the teen wants to restrict food, purge, or exercise compulsively; we say that the eating disorder is an external force that makes her do this.

Standing up to the eating disorder is easier when you are fighting not your teen but this evil intruder. Some teens find this concept helpful. It can help reduce the shame related to bingeing and purging and other undesirable behaviors. You can empathically say, "I know it's the eating disorder that makes you do this."

However, not all teens experience their eating disorder in the same way. Some can become angry when parents talk about the eating disorder as something separate from them. In such cases, it's unhelpful to use this metaphor aloud with your teen. But I encourage you to use it privately to help you feel united with your teen against a common enemy.

Closing Thoughts

In this chapter you have learned to prioritize various eating disorder and related behaviors, how to ensure the safety of your teen, and how to interrupt common eating disorder symptoms. In the next chapter, we will talk specifically about strategies to take charge of your teen's meals.

CHAPTER 5

Preparing to Implement Meals

In this chapter you'll learn how to implement structured and supervised meals to help your teen recover. You'll also learn strategies for planning meals, deciding what to serve, setting expectations for meals, and managing your teen's schedule. Please keep in mind the warning about refeeding syndrome (see chapter 3).

Planning Ahead

When providing food for a teen in recovery, you may feel overwhelmed by the sheer quantity of food you will be buying, preparing, and serving—along with the extra time it takes to do these tasks. However, with some forethought, you can prevent additional trips to the grocery store and reduce stress. Planning ahead is also usually more cost-effective than leaving food decisions to the last minute.

Once a week make the time to plan your teen's meals for the next seven days:

- Breakfast (at least two different options to alternate between)

- Lunch

- Snacks (enough for two to three a day)

- Dinner *for the entire family*

Plan a family meal for dinner with components that everyone, including your teen with an eating disorder, can eat in varying quantities. Although your teen's eating is the key focus, this will save time and move your teen toward eating what everyone else is eating—a major goal of treatment.

Try to buy everything on the shopping list at once to minimize trips to the market. Remember that if your teen needs to gain weight, he or she will commonly require a lot of food.

ONLINE ACTIVITY 6:
Weekly Meal Planning Form

To help you plan your child's meals and snacks a week at a time, download this handy form from http://www.newharbinger.com /40439. There is also space where you can jot down your shopping list.

Knowing What to Serve

You may be reassured to know that in research studies of FBT, parents are not given a meal plan or told specifically what to feed their teens. You, the parent, plan out meals based on your knowledge and experience. I believe this is common sense: you are the expert on your family. You may have other children who do not have eating disorders. And you knew how to feed your teen with an eating disorder before he became ill. So trust your parental judgment and develop meals that make sense for your family.

You should use the nutrition knowledge you have already acquired as a parent to determine what your teen should be eating. While nutritional balance is important, within broad parameters this is not the primary concern. The primary concern is that your teen is getting enough energy at meals. If you are unsure and want help planning meals, your therapist or a dietitian can help. If you enlist a dietitian, only parents should meet with him or her. Dietitians who meet directly with teens can undermine the authority of parents.

FBT encourages parents to consider the meals to be dosages of medication. If your child needed an antibiotic, would you allow your child to determine the dose? If your teen complained that the medication tasted terrible or caused a stomachache, or argued and begged you to let her skip a dose, would you yield? Of course not! You should adopt the same philosophy when determining what and how much your teen needs to eat. Food is the medicine that will promote full brain healing and ultimately allow her to recover and make independent food decisions.

When to Consult a Registered Dietitian

Although working with an eating disorder dietitian is not a traditional part of FBT, many parents who are uncertain of their child's dietary needs—or are facing specific eating challenges—find it a helpful resource. A dietitian can help plan meals to address your teen's specific needs. If he has any other medical issues impacting dietary restrictions (diabetes, a food allergy, or the like), then working with a dietitian is strongly advised.

Please find a dietitian who specializes in eating disorders and promotes neither weight loss nor rigid rules about food. One of your goals is to increase your teen's flexibility in eating, so make sure any dietitian with whom you work espouses this same philosophy. Never follow a strict meal plan or cook foods that are unnatural for your family. A dietitian can help you identify ways to make your existing recipes more calorie dense by adding certain ingredients to your child's food.

A Word About Vegetarian and Vegan Diets

One of your goals for your teen will be expanding the range of foods she eats. Allowing your teen to adopt the strictures of a vegetarian or vegan diet is a step in the wrong direction. A vegan diet is simply too restrictive for most teens, especially one recovering from an eating disorder. Nor is a vegetarian diet conducive to recovery. Unless your entire family has been vegetarian for many years before your teen developed an eating disorder, vegetarianism should be discouraged. Low-fat, low-carb, gluten-free, and nondairy diets should likewise be discouraged except in the case of a diagnosed allergy, as they often are a symptom of the disorder rather than founded in legitimate health concerns.

Although no formal research exists, many parents report that the consumption of animal fats promotes more rapid brain recovery in their teens, as exhibited by improvements in logical thinking and mood. For a family who has long been vegetarian, the equivalent would be early reintroduction of fats such as cheese, cream, and butter.

Planning Meals

As discussed in chapter 4, a structured meal plan of three meals a day plus two to three snacks is best for all types of eating disorders. If your child needs to gain weight, it will be difficult to get in enough food if you are feeding fewer than five times per day. Similarly, if you are helping to prevent your teen from bingeing, feeding at regular intervals, no more than three hours apart, is critical. Longer gaps can create an increasing urge to binge. Additionally, parents report that for teens with anorexia, resistance to eating increases when there is a gap of more than four hours between meals.

When planning meals for a teen, you generally want all macronutrient groups (starch, protein, vegetables or fruit, and fat) present in balanced proportions in each meal and snack. There are some exceptions: teens needing to gain weight need higher amounts of fat along with reduced quantities of fresh fruits and vegetables to ensure enough energy intake in a reduced volume that prevents early fullness. Teens who are prone to binge eat will especially benefit from the inclusion of starches, proteins, and fats at every meal and snack, as this will reduce urges to binge.

Early advice on weight restoration recommended to "start low and go slow" when adding calories. However, recent research has shown that, for patients not at risk for refeeding syndrome, going higher and faster leads to speedier recovery and better overall outcomes (Garber et al. 2016). Furthermore, early weight gain predicts better recovery.

Although I discourage calorie counting, a ballpark goal is helpful for many parents. Your doctor can help determine what is safe for your child. This number might be around 2,000 to 2,500 calories per day to start. If your child has been eating considerably less than this, he or she may take a few days to reach this level.

For teens needing to gain weight, the calorie goal often reaches 3,000 to 6,000 calories per day to obtain a desired weight gain goal of *at least* one to two pounds (0.5 to 1 kg) per week. Achievement of these calorie goals can be very challenging for those with anorexia nervosa due to the anxiety generated by increased intake. Understand that if you go more slowly than one to two pounds per week, recovery takes longer.

Parents and teens are often perplexed by such high calorie needs. It takes a surprising amount of energy to restore a starving body to health and rebuild everything that was depleted during the period of restriction. During the process of renourishment, individuals with anorexia nervosa often become *hypermetabolic*, meaning that their metabolism has kicked into high gear (Marzola et al. 2013). The body may convert additional calorie intake into heat rather than using it to build tissue. This paradoxical symptom makes recovery even harder. Hypermetabolism can persist for six months or more after weight restoration.

As weight is gained, the body burns more energy, so calorie needs increase further. As a result, individuals recovering from anorexia nervosa usually require escalating calorie intake to maintain a steady weight gain. Weekly weigh-ins to record progress are a prudent way to track whether calorie intake is keeping pace with the body's changing needs (more on this later in the chapter). Once a week at a minimum is helpful for tracking progress during the weight gain phase. If you are concerned, you can weigh more frequently. If and when the rate of weight gain slows or stops, calorie intake must be increased. Sometimes weight can increase in spurts, so don't immediately panic if the pace of weight gain slows one week.

Jack, a father from Oregon, recalls, "My petite girl, who was diagnosed at age fourteen and was five-foot-three, needed 3,500 calories per day for a very long time." Lourdes, a mother in Arizona, says, "We hit the 6,000-plus calorie mark just to keep up and had to stay at that level for well over two years. If we dropped down even a little, whoosh! The weight would come off."

Be cautious about the urge to cut back on calories once an individual has reached a goal weight. In my experience, teens and parents are often eager to reduce the meal plan. This often backfires and results in weight loss. It is likely your teen will continue to have elevated energy needs for some time. So be sure to keep those calorically dense foods coming.

What Food to Serve

One key meal planning challenge: the foods most teens will need to eat as part of recovery are the very foods they are frightened to eat. A recovery meal plan may require them to eat foods that they have not eaten in a very long time or that they have been bingeing on. This can be triggering and scary.

One criterion for recovery is your child's capacity to eat all the foods she used to eat approximately two to three years before showing signs of an eating disorder. This is a helpful guide to determine which foods to serve. You do not need to serve all these foods right away or even soon, but it is helpful to start the list and have a plan to cover them during the course of recovery. Your teen may insist that she doesn't like these foods anymore, or that her palate has matured and she no longer cares for rich foods or desserts. That is most likely the eating disorder talking. Ignore the disorder—add these foods to the list!

ONLINE ACTIVITY 7: Meals My Teen Used to Enjoy

It can be helpful to jot down all the foods your teen used to like before the eating disorder took hold. Download this worksheet from http://www.newharbinger.com/40439. You will also use this as a reference list against which to check progress.

Strategies to Increase Caloric Density

For teens needing to gain weight, a useful strategy is to increase the caloric density of the food they eat. This means packing the greatest energy into the smallest space. As you will discover in chapter 6, teens with restrictive eating disorders have stomachs that have literally shrunken. It is critical that their food punch above its weight calorically.

Because fat has twice the caloric density of protein and carbohydrates, enhancing the fat content of foods is a simple way to boost energy intake. Many families have used the following strategies to add caloric density to food:

- Adding protein powder or Benecalorie, a product containing a concentrated source of calories, to meals

- Adding heavy cream to eggs and sauces

- Filling out sauces, soups, egg dishes, and casseroles with other fats (canola oil, coconut oil, coconut milk, butter, cream cheese, peanut butter, almond butter, sour cream, or mayonnaise)

- Using more oil and butter when cooking

- Increasing intake of cheese, avocado, nuts, nut butters, and hummus

- Increasing intake of animal fats

- Decreasing raw vegetables and fruits, which create early fullness and gas (As a parent, it pains me to say this, but if your child needs to gain weight, fruits and vegetables are not your first choice!)

- Increasing consumption of beverages containing fats or sugar. (Replace water with milk, yogurt drinks, milkshakes, protein drinks, juice, sports drinks, or soda.)

You will need to find the correct balance to manage your teen's anxiety while adding sufficient calories. You know your teen best, and although there will be trial and error, you *will* find the right balance.

Nutritional Drinks

Many families incorporate fortified nutritional supplement drinks into their teen's meal plan. While I always think it best for teens to eat real food, there are many situations in which supplements can be invaluable. For example, in recovery's early phases your teen may offer less resistance to drinking than to eating. Also, drinks can generally be consumed more quickly than solid foods and serve for quick convenient nutrition, especially in travel situations.

These products, made by a number of different companies, contain nutrients in a calorie-dense liquid or "shake." The brands sold at grocery and drugstores in the United States include Boost and Ensure, which come in different flavors and are usually sold in plastic bottles. Some come in powder form and must be mixed with water. There are non-dairy versions known as Boost Breeze and Ensure Clear, which are packaged in juice boxes and may be ordered online. There are brands with even higher caloric density. In hospital settings, these products are used for patients who are unable to eat—due to a broken jaw, for instance—or need extra nutrition.

Six to eight ounces of these products typically have between 200 and 350 calories, depending on the brand and formulation. They taste better chilled and can be added to a meal in place of a lower-calorie beverage, used as a snack, or used in the preparation of oatmeal, smoothies, or milkshakes. In some residential centers, three nutritional supplements would be considered equivalent to a meal: if the teen refused to eat altogether, he would be offered three nutritional drinks; if the teen consumed half the meal, he would be asked to have two drinks; and if the teen ate a majority of the meal but didn't finish, he would be asked to top off with a single supplement.

Parents refeeding at home can choose whether they will offer an alternative meal or a replacement when a teen refuses to eat or finish a meal or snack. However, carefully consider adopting any feeding and eating patterns that are atypical for your family.

Common Questions Regarding Meal Planning

Here are some common questions parents have regarding meals.

Should I Be Honest About the Addition of Fats to My Child's Food?

Teens ask persistently and very directly about what's in their food. They will ultimately find the cream in the fridge or hear the butter dish being opened. Anxious teens sometimes go through the kitchen trash and look for empty food containers.

I suggest neither directly lying about fat content nor offering the information. In other words, don't volunteer to your teen that you are adding heavy whipping cream to every sauce you serve. Take out the trash frequently, don't take him shopping with you, and, if asked, simply say, "It's not helpful to discuss what goes into your food. Trust me. I know exactly what you need right now." If possible, keep your teen out of the kitchen to avoid increased anxiety.

A caveat is for those teens whose calorie needs remain very high while transitioning to eating without parental supervision, such as when they go off to college. These teens can inadvertently lose weight because they didn't realize the oatmeal prepared at home was made with heavy whipping cream instead of water. In this case, disclosure of ingredients would need to be relayed before your teen goes to college.

Should I Measure Food?

I don't recommend measuring food. This is an eating disorder behavior we want your teen to abandon. However, if you are following a meal plan or calorie suggestions, it can be helpful to measure foods discreetly at the outset, but only until you get a feel for the portions necessary. At that point, I recommend that you switch to eyeballing and estimating amounts. This is the behavior you want your teen to emulate; you do not want her to show up in the dining hall with measuring spoons and cups.

Should Everyone Eat the Same Food?

It is not necessary to eat exactly the same foods as your recovering teen. I think it is realistic to model that every person has different nutritional needs. When your teen was a baby, you did not eat baby food with him. In general, teens need to eat more than their middle-aged parents. That said, there is great value in modeling the eating behaviors your teen fears. A great strategy is to make a meal with components. If your meal is spaghetti and meatballs, salad, and garlic bread, everyone will have some of each of these foods, but the amounts can vary. Your growing teen with an eating disorder may need more spaghetti, meatballs, and garlic bread, but less salad, than you do.

Should I Order Prepared Food to Ensure Sufficient Calories?

Today it is easy to buy foods with a known calorie content. Despite the convenience of this, I think it is a better strategy to primarily cook at home. Many teens with eating disorders are whizzes at counting calories based on portion sizes and will cling to information gleaned from restaurant calorie counts or the labels on packaged dinners. They may even grow to resist eating foods unless their nutritional content is available. Therefore, it is better if you can keep your teen from knowing exactly how many calories you are serving by cooking from scratch at least some of the time. Casseroles, soups, and the like are great for getting your teen used to eating foods with a more indeterminate calorie content.

Structuring Mealtime

To deliver your teen's primary medication—an effective meal plan— you need to establish a structure and expectation that she will eat. Remember that your home is now effectively a residential treatment center for one patient. Most patients in residential treatment centers are neither tube fed nor fed against their will. However, they *are* required to eat. Centers establish a tightly controlled structure. Meals and snacks are prioritized and occur at regular times in a regular place. Patients are expected to eat within a specified time frame. Until they complete the meal, they are not allowed to proceed to the next activity. If they do not complete the meal, there is a consequence.

You will want to apply the same level of discipline and expectation in your home. Meals and snacks should follow a schedule and have a time limit. In chapter 6, I will discuss what to do if your child cannot complete a meal within a time limit.

Require Your Teen to Eat

Remember that your teen may have a voice in his head that berates him for eating anything "fattening" or unhealthy. It is hard for a teen to defy that voice. Your insistence that your child eat more than he intends and eat foods that the eating disorder instructed him to refuse is an act not of control but of *kindness*—you are giving your teen permission to eat. Teen patients have confessed to me, "When my parents made me eat that food, part of me really wanted it." Outwardly, they may continue to protest, insisting they do not like the food and are only humoring you.

Felicia, a mother from Georgia, recounts:

> In the beginning, when we started giving our daughter a daily shake, it was really hard. We tried to offer different flavors, but she would only have strawberry. The eating disorder in her head told her that at least it is a "fruit." Every day she would say, "Just do not give me chocolate, Mom." Well, after a few months we gave her a chocolate shake and it was not fun. There was lots of screaming and crying, but eventually she drank it. Months later she said to me, "I was so glad when you gave me that chocolate shake and made me eat it. My eating disorder did not want me to have chocolate but I wanted chocolate so bad!"

Do not lose heart and never underestimate the power of what you are doing.

Remove Choices About What to Eat

Choice can be difficult for those with eating disorders. When faced with food options, their brains are easily overwhelmed. The eating disorder thoughts get so intense that they cannot rationally decide. The eating disorder may desperately calculate the lowest-calorie option—which, most of the time, is to just avoid eating altogether.

Removing all food choices actually reduces anxiety. This is why in FBT, contrary to traditional hospital practices, meal planning is done *without* consulting the child. Parents decide what their children eat. One popular concept is the *magic plate*: the parents prepare and plate the food and present the teen with the plate. All the teen has to do is eat. Other members of the family may continue to make their own plates if this is typical for the family.

Maintaining a Schedule

Maintaining a structured meal schedule, even on the weekends, can be essential for your teen's recovery. This may require you to wake your teen for breakfast at a consistent time, even on the weekends. It can also require significant limitations on your teen's activities. Lost meals mean slower recovery.

Managing School Schedules and Meals

Supervision of snacks and lunches during the school day should receive important consideration. A typical school day spans one meal and two snacks. This is a significant portion of your teen's daily intake. Failure to eat these meals could hinder recovery. If you did not see your child eating what you have packed, you must assume it has not been eaten. How do families handle this?

Options include any combination of the following:

- Teen attends school only part of the day and eats lunch at home

- Parent goes to school to supervise the eating of snacks and lunch in a private office

- Parent drives to school and the teen meets the parent to eat in the car before returning to class

- Parent volunteers at the school and can incidentally supervise meals and snacks

- Another adult at the school—a favorite teacher, school nurse, special education teacher, or administrator—is designated to supervise meals and snacks (see below for special considerations regarding such arrangements)

Be creative—there are many possible solutions! Just take care to adopt a strategy that protects your teen from any embarrassment caused by being seen with you at school.

If another adult supervises on your behalf, be sure to provide guidelines. Many teens with eating disorders will dump part of their lunch and then show up with only a portion of what was packed at home. You will want the supervisor to know exactly what your teen is supposed to eat. You may want to have a standard meal and relay it: "Her lunch will always contain a sandwich, a drink, chips, and yogurt." Or you can send a daily email detailing what is packed so the supervisor can verify that all items have been eaten. Alternatively, you can deliver the packed lunch directly to the school office each morning to prevent tampering.

The supervisor should not be expected to have the skills to make your teen eat—only to report back to you. You will need to let the supervisor know how to handle things if your child doesn't complete the lunch and what he or she should do if your teen exhibits trouble during the meal (the supervisor should relay any problematic behaviors and send uneaten food home so it can be made up).

Consider who will prepare and supervise all of your child's meals and where they will be eaten. In general, a child should not be put in charge of her own meals until she can do so without eating disorder behaviors. Until then, I believe it is the parents' job to manage the meals. Your child may have little or no motivation to get better and may be struggling with very strong urges. The promise of future independence, including the opportunity to eat unsupervised or out with friends, may sometimes be the best or only motivator for a teen to eat appropriately.

ONLINE ACTIVITY 8:
Responsibility for Meals and Snacks

Creating a weekly schedule of who will prepare all of your child's meals and snacks, and who will supervise your child when eating them, is crucial to recovery. Download this planner from http://www.newharbinger.com/40439 to stay organized.

Taking Time off from School

At the outset, you should address whether your teen should take time off from school. In many instances, the best-case scenario is for parents to pull a teen out of school for a short time to establish the importance of regular eating and to supervise all meals and snacks. In more severe cases, you can consider homeschooling. Doing so can kick-start the recovery with an intensity and level of attention equal to the severity of the disorder.

Pulling your teen out of school serves a number of specific functions:

- It allows your teen to focus solely on the most important issue—getting healthy—because the distraction and pressures of school have been removed.

- It can provide relief for all involved when the stress of eating is not compounded by the stress of school.

- It sends an important message that the teen's health will be prioritized above everything else.

- It allows you to establish a routine of regular supervised meals.

- It gives time to supervise meals that may initially go slowly without having to worry about the starting bell.

- It gives you social leverage and gives your teen a goal toward which to work.

When meals are going smoothly and there is a reduction in binge-ing and purging, your teen will be ready to return to school to see friends.

Taking Away Activities

There may be activities other than school from which you need to pull your teen. Physical education, sports, school trips, and food-related social events usually top this list. You may be apprehensive about taking these activities away from your child. You might even say to yourself, "It *will kill* her to miss this." Here's what eating disorder activist Laura Collins Lyster-Mensh advises:

> Parents, any time you are afraid to do the right thing because you think it might crush their spirit, make things worse, cause more resistance, be too big a fuss, or disappoint them so much they might lose their will to live...remember that what "will kill" is the illness. Giving in to an eating disorder for any reason is what "will kill." (2011)

Regular Weigh-ins

If your teen needs to gain weight, regular weigh-ins to measure prog-ress are critical. Even if he does not need to gain weight, weigh-ins remain useful in evaluating the impact of your meal plan and deter-mining if your teen is in his healthy weight range. If he is still growing, it also allows you to measure whether his weight is keeping pace (see chapter 3).

Weight Tracker

Keeping track of your teen's weight on a weekly basis is essential to measuring his health. Record the weigh-ins on the downloadable chart available at http://www.newharbinger.com/40439.

Many teens with restrictive eating disorders may manipulate their weights, making it tricky to get an accurate measure. Strategies I have seen to make themselves appear heavier include:

- Water-loading—drinking large quantities of water prior to weigh-ins

- Secreting weights, cell phones, rocks, coins, or other small heavy items in pockets, underwear, bras, and, in extreme cases, body cavities

- Wearing extra layers of clothes

If your teen is manipulating weight, you will likely grow wise. To get an accurate weight, have her urinate before being weighed (and have a lab measure the urine for the dilution characteristic of water-loading). Also have your child completely undress in front of a parent or professional and then change into a gown. You may also need to schedule surprise weigh-ins at the pediatrician's office—no warning means no opportunity to hide items in clothes or to water-load.

Blind or Open Weigh-ins?

Traditionally, many doctors treating eating disorders withhold the results of patients' weights from them as an anxiety-management strategy. In contrast, with FBT the therapist weighs clients weekly, and the weight is shared with both the teen and the parents. This provides exposure, acclimating the teen to the feared situation and encouraging distress tolerance. Receiving the weight report within a therapeutic setting, rather than by chancing upon a scale at a friend's house, provides the teen greater emotional support. It keeps everyone—including the teen—on the same page and demonstrates the food intake required to achieve a healthy weight range. Finally, open weighing offers important timely feedback to the parents on the results of their meal implementation. For a teen needing to gain weight, the desired rate is one to two pounds (0.5 to 1 kilogram) per week. If this is not happening, parents need to know and adjust their meal plans accordingly.

For these reasons, I think it is best to weigh openly and share the weights with both parents and teens. That said, in cases where anxiety is extremely high, it might be better to withhold weight from a teen during recovery's early stages. Sometimes we must prioritize weight gain in the near term, knowing we can face the anxiety later. As recovery continues, it becomes more adaptive for the teen to know and accept his weight. Your teen will need this data when he applies for a driver's license, for instance, and will eventually find access to a scale somewhere.

If you are not working with an FBT therapist, think about who will weigh your teen. It can be a medical doctor or registered dietitian. As a last resort, you can do it at home, although this can place parents in a tough spot. Weighing on a weekly basis will suffice, unless directed otherwise by a medical doctor.

Meal Suggestions

Don't know where to start when it comes to meal planning? See http://www.newharbinger.com/40439 for meal ideas from my colleague, Katie Grubiak, a registered dietitian nutritionist. She provides numerous tips for tailoring common meals to meet a variety of energy needs and palates.

Closing Thoughts

In this chapter we have focused on food, specifically how to structure meals, what food to serve, and how to monitor weight gain, if that is a goal. You can now plan meals that will restore your teen to health.

CHAPTER 6

Mealtime Strategies

Initially, most parents find it *very* difficult to turn food refusal into acceptance. But there is no other road to recovery. Here's the good news: as a parent of a teen, you already have volumes of experience getting your teen to do various things she rejected at first. You can call upon this body of experience. Think about strategies you've used to get your teen to take medicine, clean up her room, clear the dishes, and so on. These same strategies can be applied to getting her to eat. While it seems improbable, you—the parents—are the ideal people to achieve this. But *how?*

In this chapter, you'll learn specific strategies for handling mealtimes, including ways to manage your teen's eating anxiety and tactics for encouraging meal completion. Many of the incentives that can be used to encourage eating can also be used to limit other eating disorder behaviors. You will see in this chapter that there is no single way to do things. Every family is different; it is important to figure out what works for your teen.

Setting Mealtime Expectations

Preestablishing ground rules for mealtimes will facilitate the renourishment process. Many parents have found it helpful to set a rule: *Life stops until you eat.* Until a meal is completed, the teen may not proceed to the next activity, whether it be school, time with friends, or a family outing. Some parents find that keeping their teen at the table until he has eaten truly reinforces the message that there is no other choice than to disobey the eating disorder's demands. Alternatively, in order to avoid what can become marathon eating sessions and keep to a tighter schedule, some parents find it helpful to impose a time limit on meals. Treatment centers often suggest a thirty-minute time limit for meals and a fifteen-minute time limit for snacks. If meals are not completed in this time, they initiate consequences, which are discussed later in this chapter.

Use the following questions to help establish guidelines for mealtime setting and behavior:

Who will be at the meal?

If there is a problem, how will it be handled? Will it be discussed during the meal or later?

What is the plan if my child doesn't eat?

What if my child refuses to eat certain types of food?

You may not have the answers to these questions yet, but give it a try. Your ground rules may need to evolve as you experiment and discover what works best in your household, but it is important to have a plan in advance of meals, when your teen's anxiety will be highest. The goal is to discover what works for you, not to test strategies that have worked for other families. You may also notice that thinking about these questions increases your own anxiety; this is normal. Chapter 7 discusses strategies for parents to use when you find yourself getting anxious, overwhelmed, or mad.

Start at Home

It is usually best to start treatment by eating most, if not all, meals at home. Your teen's anxiety may be elevated, and she may act unpredictably when presented with food. Teens have been known to scream, throw food, run out of the room, and rub food in parents' hair. In a public setting, it will be harder to stand up to the eating disorder and require your teen to eat. The safety, privacy, and controlled environment of the home is a better place to face these behaviors. Over time, as parental and teen skills and behaviors improve, you can introduce other eating environments and work on generalizing skills to other settings, such as restaurants and friends' houses.

Using Distractions

Some teenagers benefit from the use of distractions. For some teens, distractions are most needed *before* the meal, when parents are preparing food and anxiety about the upcoming meal is high. Some teens will loiter around the kitchen to determine what you are putting in their food. It is best to keep your child out of the kitchen and reject any input on what you are preparing. Encourage your child to engage in an activity, such as watching television, doing a puzzle book, playing a video game, coloring, or doing a craft project. Recruiting one adult to be the distractor while another prepares meals can prevent stress.

For some teens, anxiety peaks *during* the meal, when distractions can expedite meal completion. Distractions of this kind may include any activity that does not prevent eating, such as:

- Watching television

- Listening to podcasts, music, or an audiobook

- Conversing about topics other than food and the eating disorder

- Telling jokes (that are not weight-based)

- Working on puzzles (crosswords, word search, sudoku) or word games (Twenty Questions, Would You Rather?, Ghost)

- Playing cards, dominoes, or board games (if a tablet is available, game apps are more manageable during meals than games with pieces)

Monitor closely to ensure that these distractions are facilitating rather than impeding eating.

Some teens, especially those who binge or purge, may have more anxiety *after* the meal. They benefit from parents who engage them in activities afterward, when the eating disorder is torturing them. Many of the same activities helpful before or during a meal will work afterward as well.

Ways to Encourage Eating (and Manage Other Behaviors)

Setting rules and boundaries creates safety for your teen and demonstrates that you are not afraid of the eating disorder, that you know what you are doing, and that you can see the bigger picture. Offering rewards and giving consequences can often be successful strategies. But it is best to develop them before you sit down for the meal.

The most effective incentives are generally tied to a specific measurable behavior, such as the completion of a meal or a number of meals, completion of meals without eating disorder behaviors (such as hiding or disassembling food), avoiding the kitchen when parents are preparing food, not needing multiple reminders to come to the table, or not smearing food. It is less effective to tie rewards to an outcome over which the teen does not have direct control, such as a five-pound weight gain (over which those serving the food have more control).

Logical consequences—not punishments but results that follow the behavior in a logical way—are always best. For example, if your teen refuses to eat breakfast, keeping her home from school is a proportionate response: teens cannot effectively concentrate in school without nutrition for their brains. If you catch your teen exercising in the shower, it makes sense to put her on bed rest, which you can do in the most loving way possible: "I'm so sorry, but your body is depleted and now you must conserve what little fuel your body has left." Supplementing an incomplete meal with more food or a supplemental shake is a logical way to make up for lost calories. Logical consequences should be immediate—telling her that she can't go to summer camp next month holds little benefit in the moment. I encourage you to come up with your own logical consequences for the behaviors you want to address. Be creative!

Early in recovery, your teen may be in low spirits and uninterested in doing much, so it can sometimes be hard to come up with motivating rewards. Furthermore, there is some evidence that the brains of individuals with anorexia nervosa do not process rewards in the same way as people without anorexia nervosa (Bischoff-Grethe et al. 2013). As a result, they may perceive a given perk as less motivating than do other people. Despite these difficulties, for many teens with eating disorders, school is a positive environment and can serve as a reward, as can time with friends. Use of electronics is another valuable incentive for most teens.

One word of caution: all rewards and consequences "lose their shine" over time. This is important, as it shows that your teen is learning and using new behaviors. Once a behavior becomes easy, you should stop rewarding it and set a new goal. You may need to return to this chapter to think about new and different strategies.

Positive reinforcements should be used whenever possible—they are generally more motivating than either negative consequences or the loss of freedoms. The most effective consequences depend on the age and nature of your child. The lists below provide some ideas for positive reinforcements and negative consequences.

Positive reinforcements

School

Time with friends

Points toward a family day trip or mini-vacation

Special time with a pet

Visit from a favorite relative or family friend

Watching a movie from a list your child has created in advance

Watching the next episode in a television series

Reading the next chapter in a book you are reading aloud as a family

Time on a family project (art, puzzle, home improvement, etc.)

Participating in a family activity or game right after a meal

Special family outing or activity

Mobile phone or electronic devise use (sometimes you may need to take it away to let your teen earn it back)

Foreign-language lesson

Makeup

Money for music

Streaming video

Driving lessons

Stickers or points that can be accrued to earn any of the above

Negative consequences

The addition of food to the next meal to make up for incomplete meals

One-on-one meals in a private room, instead of family meals

Twenty-four hours of rest after any food refusal, even if eventually compliant

Bed rest to conserve energy

Going to the hospital for fluids

Respite care or residential treatment

Loss of any of the positive consequences

Use of a supplemental nutrition shake (either homemade or commercially available) for incomplete meals

More supervision throughout the day

More one-on-one time with family

Another scheduled snack

Milkshake with meals

Homeschooling

Additional therapy

One positive reinforcement with which to take caution is time for exercise. This is best used later in recovery and is not advisable if your teen has medical restrictions or is obsessive about exercise.

How to Get Your Teen to Actually Eat at Mealtimes

As mentioned earlier in this chapter, most teens with eating disorders regard the meal before them with high anxiety. The atmosphere at mealtimes can be tense. No amount of convincing them that there's nothing to fear seems to help, because nervous systems in a state of activation cannot think logically.

Instead, parents must directly address their symptoms of anxiety and fear. In a seeming paradox, food is the medicine that will ultimately make them less afraid of food. Families can make meals bearable and provide an environment that allows teenagers with eating disorders to recover and flourish. Research on the family meal (White et al. 2015), as well as the experience of staff at residential treatment centers and parents' reports, highlights some strategies that encourage meal completion. Below are ways you can help.

Stay calm. When your teen is riding a wave of anxiety, you want to stay on the shore and calm her down—not join her in the surf. This is easier said than done, but getting upset will only further raise her anxiety and make it even harder for her to eat. Staying calm is a parental super-power you probably remember from when your toddler had a meltdown in the cereal aisle.

Be confident. Calm and confident parents inspire trust in their children, making it easier for them to eat. If you're unsure, frazzled, or showing fear, your teen will take your cue. Desist from complaining about how hard it is on you too—he needs you to be competent and unflappable. If you are not capable of internal confidence and calm, fake it until you are.

Give physical support. Try sitting right next to your teen during meal-times. If there are two parents at the meal, one parent should sit on each side of her. You may want to even lean in close. It is an act of love to share that space and support a child through a meal when she is ter-rified. Consider having a parent sit at the chair nearest the door to discourage leaving the table. But physical restraint is almost never war-ranted except when your teen is in physical danger. There are always other ways to respond.

Eat the food you are asking your teen to eat. If your teen is terrified of eating meat, seeing people around him eat it can sometimes alleviate fear. As discussed previously, you do not need to eat exactly what your teen is eating. To the extent that you do, it sends a message that these foods are safe.

Use verbal prompts. These may be direct or indirect. Examples of direct verbal prompts include instructions, such as, "You need to eat your sandwich." "Pick it up and eat it." "Start with your sandwich." "Take another bite." "I want you to take a bigger bite." Indirect prompts are comments that encourage or suggest eating, such as, "Keep going" or "Eat some more."

Use physical prompts. Physical prompts include actions such as pushing a plate of food toward the teen, handing her a fork, or putting food on the fork and handing it to her. Such actions by parents can make the process of eating psychologically easier for the teen by remov-ing the element of choice.

Validate. When you hear your teen say he doesn't want to eat, it is more helpful to simply listen and stay calm than it is to argue or reason with him. You can even say, "I understand that you don't want to eat. I hear you."

Be reassuring. Empathize with your child's fear or anxiety, and express confidence that she will be okay. Say, "I know you are scared, and I also know you can do this." If your teen responds well to playful teasing, by all means try some humor! Just be reassuring and supportive. She may respond to your reassurance with derision or hostility, but it is probably helping anyway.

Use a mantra. This can keep you from getting pulled into an argument about what your teen is eating and can also be calming for you. Recite something like, "Yes, I know this is hard…I love you." Greer, a mother from Australia, reports, "The mantras are helpful at times, and I found them more helpful for myself in the moment. My daughter would throw a plate at my head or spit at me, and I would robotically get up, get a new plate, replace the food, and say, 'Food is your medicine. I am stronger than the eating disorder.' It helped me to stay strong."

Stay quiet. Sometimes the best response is no response or just "Mmm-hmm." It relieves the parent of having to come up with fresh responses and doesn't give the teen anything to argue with. It can be calming for all.

Do it together. The presence and support of parents, siblings, and extended family during and after meals are often helpful and normalizing. If possible, have everyone eat together. When anxiety is very high and there are many difficult behaviors to manage, this may not be possible, but the goal should be to return the family to some semblance of family meals, which offer several long-term benefits for your child's healthy development. If you did not have the habit of family meals before the illness, create rituals and new family customs around them.

Resist the urge to reason. One of the greatest challenges parents face at mealtimes is resisting the urge to reason with their child. But this you must do. A teen who makes good and logical choices in other areas of his life may be totally unreasonable when it comes to food, exercise, or the body. You will never win a mealtime debate with an eating disorder. Parents should avoid the common trap of getting stuck in the content of their child's anxious thoughts. But if this were easy to do, we wouldn't need this book!

Master the art of redirection. It is difficult to refrain from responding to what your teen says. But when you try to reason with the content of your child's thoughts, it leads to arguing and conflict. Instead, when you can address the fears and anxieties behind the thoughts, you provide support. This empathy can take time to develop; the examples that follow may help point you in the right direction.

Your teen says: "I can't eat bread. Bread is bad for you."

Argumentative response: "You need starches. You like bread."

What your teen means: "I'm scared to eat bread."

Supportive response: "I know it's hard for you. I know you're scared. I'm here with you."

Your teen says: "How many calories are in this ice cream? There's too much fat in it."

Argumentative response: "It's not that many calories. You can eat fat. Don't you want to get well?"

What your teen means: "I'm scared to eat this ice cream."

Supportive response: "I know you are scared. I'm eating the ice cream with you. This is exactly what you need."

Your teen says: "This is too much food. I can't possibly eat all of it. I won't eat it all."

Argumentative response: "It's not that much food. It's only one serving of each portion. I'll check and make sure; maybe it's not right."

What your teen means: "I'm scared to eat this. I don't trust that you know what to give me. I'm scared of being fat."

Supportive response: "This is exactly the right amount of food. I know what you need."

Your teen says: "I'm not hungry. I won't eat this."

Argumentative response: "You must eat this or you can't _____ ."

What your teen means: "I'm scared to eat this."

Supportive response: "I know this is hard. It's time to eat."

Your teen says: "If I eat this I won't be able to control myself and will eat too much."

Argumentative response: "Everyone at home eats this. You need to learn how to eat it and keep it down."

What your teen means: "I'm scared this food will make me lose control."

Supportive response: "I will help you eat the right amount, and I will stay with you to make sure you don't have too much."

Have a plan for unfinished meals. Not every mealtime strategy will work, and you will undoubtedly need to have a range of alternatives. Use any of the following or come up with your own creative backup plans when your teen doesn't finish a meal:

- End the meal and add additional food to the next meal.

- Take a break and resume the meal when everyone is calmer.

- Substitute the dinner with a preapproved and planned supplement, milkshake, or replacement meal that will help sustain your teen without giving in to the eating disorder.

- If time limits prove unhelpful, try staying at the table for as long as it takes your teen to eat.

- Recognize that sometimes a meal will not be completed and that the teen needs to see you follow through on consequences (such as keeping him home from school or taking away his phone). Seeing that you mean business will make him more likely to complete the next meal.

Have a clear plan for meals that are refused in their entirety. Early on, work out a plan with your treatment team for what to do if a meal is refused, especially in early recovery. Many medical providers will arrange for fluids, supplements, or even tube feeds in the case of a missed meal or series of meals.

What Not to Do During Meals

You may be tempted to praise your child or threaten negative consequences in an attempt to get him to eat. However, these approaches are typically not effective at getting teens with eating disorders to eat. Here are some precautions during mealtimes:

- **Refrain from reiterating positive incentives.** The correct time to establish incentives is *outside* of meals. You might say, "If you finish the meal, you can see your friends later" or "If you gain weight, you can go back to horseback riding." Reminding your child of rewards that can be earned by finishing the meal *while* she is eating is an ineffective counter to the anxiety of the moment.

- **Avoid reiterating negative consequences or making threats.** While it is very tempting, reiterating negative consequences or the removal of privileges *during* meals is rarely effective. These messages—"If you don't eat that, you can't go to school" or "If you don't finish your toast, you'll have to eat an extra snack later"—are usually perceived as threats, increase anxiety, and make it harder to eat.

- **Don't ask your teen what or whether he wants to eat.** When you ask a teen with an eating disorder "Do you want some potatoes?" or "Do you want more?" or "Which do you want?" you're really asking the eating disorder for permission to eat. The answer will usually be no.

- **Don't provide nutritional information.** You may be doing this without even realizing it when you say, "Your body needs fat" or "Milk will make your bones strong." It is tempting to want your teen to understand why he should eat, but his logical brain is not accessible during an episode of anxious arousal.

- **Refrain from providing too much praise.** Ironically, when praised about their eating, many teens with eating disorders feel guiltier and more upset. In their minds, if they have pleased their parents, they have betrayed the eating disorder.

- **Do not negotiate.** The old warning against negotiating with a terrorist applies to negotiating with an eating disorder: doing so legitimizes and strengthens the adversary. In my experience, parents who allow a teen to negotiate what she is eating are reinforcing and empowering the eating disorder. Your teen may try to negotiate during meals. She may say, "I will eat this but not this" or "I won't eat this, but give me something else instead." An eating disorder is like a petulant child. If you give in once, the eating disorder has learned it can get you to back down; next time it will mount a stronger attack. I recommend not negotiating—holding fast seems to extinguish this behavior. However, if a pattern of negotiation has been established, some parents have been successful in extinguishing it by engaging in compassionate persistence skills or by instituting consequences in response to specific attempts by the teen to negotiate. For example, parents may establish the rule that the teen eats what she is served and that if she tries to negotiate she must eat an additional serving or lose a freedom.

ONLINE ACTIVITY 9:
Rewards and Consequences to Use with My Teen

It can be helpful to make a list of potential rewards and consequences you can use with your child. To get started, visit http://www.newharbinger.com/40439 and download this worksheet.

How to Monitor and Supervise Meals

Eating disorders can become devious during meals, so it is important to remain alert both during and after meals. Some teens, desperate to avoid the anxiety of eating, will engage in behaviors to avoid eating or minimize their intake. Behaviors to watch out for include:

- Throwing food away when parents aren't looking

- Dropping food on the ground

- Feeding food to the dog

- Putting food in plants

- Smearing food on clothing, napkins, the underside of tables, and so on

- Holding food in their cheeks and spitting it out right after meals

- Convincing siblings to eat or hide their food

- Hiding food inside their clothes—long sleeves are a good hiding place but even underwear provides coverage; also watch out for hoodies!

- Palming food during mealtime and then secreting it in their room

- Watering down open juice bottles in the refrigerator

When you are supervising your teen's meals, watch closely to ensure that he is eating and swallowing the food. Take caution if you get up or get distracted for any reason. Precautions some parents have had to take to address the above behaviors include the following:

- Disallowing the use of napkins

- Putting up their hair

- Locking up dogs during mealtimes

- Having teens dress in a tank top and shorts with no obvious hiding places

- Requiring them to show an empty mouth before leaving the table

- Serving messy foods that are harder to secret away (bread and sandwiches are easy to hide—spaghetti and meatballs, less so)

The avoidance and deception differ from other disciplinary issues. They are driven by desperation and fear, not mischief or lack of respect for you. Remember: you are fighting the eating disorder with your child—not being mean or suspicious. Be sympathetic but unapologetic.

It's Normal for Teens to Become Upset During Meals

Do not evaluate the success of your efforts based on how your teen feels or what she says. If you have followed the strategies above, do not expect your teen to thank you. Your objective is that she eats. Research shows that the strategies parents use successfully to get teens with eating disorders to eat produce more negative feelings in the teen in the short term (White et al. 2015). Your teen may become upset and make negative, even hostile, comments. Neither get discouraged nor change the plan based on their emotions. Some teens become agitated during meals, throw food, or show aggression (as discussed in chapter 4). In these cases, parents will often prepare extra food in anticipation of losing some and having to start all over again. Some parents use only paper plates.

This behavior is more likely an expression of your teen's illness than a reflection of your tactics. They may even be a sign that you are successfully challenging the eating disorder. You need to persist despite your child's potential negative reactions.

Tummy Troubles and Early Fullness

Many teens, especially those who have been restricting intake, will complain about nausea, bloating, stomachaches, hard or infrequent bowel movements, and fullness after eating only a small portion of food.

After significant weight loss, the stomach empties much more slowly than normal; this condition is called *gastroparesis*. Part of a meal may remain in the stomach for hours and hours, leading to painful bloating, fullness, nausea, and even involuntary vomiting. Movement through the large intestine is also slowed, resulting in constipation. (Normally, people have bowel movements anywhere from several times a day to several times a week; less than that is constipation. Hard stools or "pebbles" also indicate constipation. This is due to increased reabsorption of fluid in the colon due to slow transit.) Generally, these symptoms improve significantly after a few weeks of regular eating, although recovery may take months.

While this discomfort is real, it usually is neither cause for alarm nor justification for your teen to leave her meal unfinished. That said, if your teen complains of severe stomach pains or discomfort after meals, take the complaints seriously and seek a doctor's help. As long as you've consulted a medical professional and no other problems are found, do not retreat from requiring your teen to eat. As with almost every other symptom, the solution is food.

The high-fiber diets often preferred by individuals with eating disorders can make these symptoms worse. As discussed in chapter 5, eating foods with higher caloric density can help, as can making sure intake is divided into three meals and two to three snacks. Some teens report relief with heat pads or hot water bottles (wrapped in an insulating cloth) placed on their stomach after meals. You can also check with your doctor about whether any medications might be helpful for gas or constipation.

Have Compassion for Your Teen and Yourself

When your teen is having difficulty eating it is easy to become upset, frustrated, and angry. The situation can easily escalate. Unfortunately, your distress will only further raise your teen's own already elevated anxiety, making it harder for him to eat.

Showing distress does not mean that you've failed, just that you can try the next time to remain calmer. When this happens, it can be helpful to apologize to your teen for reacting with frustration instead of having listened to him. This authentic act models that it is okay not only to be imperfect but also to own your imperfections.

You may also want to try meditating or another calming technique.

Guided Meditations

Eva Musby, the parent of a child with an eating disorder, has developed some guided meditations to help parents achieve a state of calm before mealtime. You can access these recordings on her website, http://anorexiafamily.com.

It helps to show your teen compassion and love. Once threatened, eating disorders commonly make teens angry, hostile, and threatening. They may even make your teen blame *you* for ruining her life—by simply requiring that she eats! Remember: it is the eating disorder that is dangerous and threatening to ruin your teen's life—not the food, and not you. Do not believe for a moment that you are abusing your child by helping her perform a basic task that she cannot do. You are challenging the eating disorder, and this is making the eating disorder angry.

Maintaining a compassionate stance is difficult, but doing so can help your teen immensely. Meal supervision should be viewed as a caring behavior, not a controlling one. It is an act of love that requires persistence and commitment, and it may save your teen's life.

You must also show kindness to yourself. Forgive yourself if you are unable to perform meal supervision at this time. Breaks may be necessary; to get a respite, some parents send their teen to residential or day treatment programs for a few weeks or months. This is not a sign of failure or weakness. The most important thing for your loved one is to keep moving toward recovery. Your teen will eventually come home, and you can resume when she is further along in recovery. There is no perfect way to treat your child's eating disorder. By reading this book, you are taking the responsible act of acknowledging the problem and committing to take action.

Closing Thoughts

In this chapter, you have learned strategies—including distractions, rewards, and consequences—to manage mealtime anxiety and increase eating compliance. Learning different ways to help your teen combat the eating disorder provides the entire family with relief and also helps teach your teen important strategies for self-regulation. Learning ways to address behaviors, rather than getting upset with your teen, will make you more effective in your parenting life post–eating disorder.

CHAPTER 7

Assessing Progress and Managing Common Challenges

Now that you have a plan to address the eating disorder behaviors and have been supervising meals, you may feel like you have hit your stride. Or you may still find that every day is a struggle. Regardless, you are likely wondering how long you're going to have to do this and having fantasies about sending your teen away to be fixed by professionals. In this chapter, we will discuss how long it may take to recover from an eating disorder and how to determine whether you are making progress. We will also review common challenges faced by parents and some strategies for managing those.

How Long Does Full Recovery Take?

According to the FBT treatment manual, recovery can sometimes occur within one year. When speedy diagnosis has allowed an early intervention, this may be possible. Unfortunately, based on my own experience and the reports of many parents, this is not always the case. More frequently, it can take several years to escape the clutches of an eating disorder in full bloom.

An understanding of the order of symptom remission illustrates why recovery takes so long. Even accounting for different treatments and symptoms among patients, the stages of recovery from an eating disorder follow a common pattern, as demonstrated in several studies (Clausen 2004; Le Grange et al. 2012; Lock et al. 2005; Couturier and Lock 2006). Here is a summary of the time frames in which symptoms often seem to remit:

- **Remission of eating disorder behaviors.** Research on patients with bulimia nervosa shows that binge eating and purging behaviors remit at an average of *eight or nine months.*

- **Weight recovery.** For teens with anorexia, weight recovery takes on average *12 months.*

- **Psychological recovery.** Weight recovery and the absence of bingeing and purging do not mean that the eating disorder is gone. Weight recovery and behavioral changes appear to be prerequisites for psychological recovery. Eating disorder thoughts—the preoccupation with shape and weight, as well as urges to restrict, binge, purge, or exercise—will often persist for *nearly a year after your child has reached a normal weight, stopped engaging in behaviors, or both.*

While research suggests these general time frames, it has been observed that teens with high levels of obsessive-compulsive features related to eating may be relatively slower to recover. Lock and colleagues hypothesize that these patients "are more challenging for parents to redirect and thereby might take longer to change" (2005, 638). Highly anxious children often take longer to generalize their recovery skills from one situation to the next. This means that if your teen showed signs before the onset of the eating disorder of being inflexible, obsessive, or anxious, expect recovery to take longer than a year *after* weight has been stabilized and behaviors have stopped.

Practically, the slow pace of remission means that parents must keep their teens in weight and behavioral recovery—holding the scaffolding around their teens, staying vigilant, and intervening if necessary to ensure they maintain weight and do not engage in eating disorder behaviors—for an extended period, usually at least a year, to achieve full psychological recovery and brain healing. Because their eating disorder thoughts and negative body image are often still present, teens will usually want to restrict or overexercise for quite some time.

The good news is that once you complete the challenging early phase of parent-directed treatment and establish a routine, holding your teen in recovery generally becomes easier than it is during those first few weeks—that is, as long as you don't rush to return control to your teen. Some teens may not be ready to take charge of their eating for a few years. Accepting this reality will grant you the patience to hand back control slowly. Return to the stages we discussed in the eating independence continuum in chapter 3. I have known families who have needed to spend an extended amount of time in stages 2, 3, 4, or 5, retaining full or almost full supervision, before starting to return some independence over eating to the teen. As you will see in chapter 9, you can conduct experiments along the way to test and offer your teen the opportunity to demonstrate her readiness.

How to Gauge Progress

Now that you have taken charge of meals for your teen and interrupted problematic behaviors, you will want to assess progress. How do you know whether your interventions are working? As we've discussed, your teen won't be complimenting you on the great job you've been doing. While that would be nice, I argue that the measure of your success is often the intensity of your teen's negative emotional reaction around meals or after you've interrupted an eating disorder behavior.

It can be hard to tell whether you are making headway in the lengthy war against an eating disorder. You may lose specific battles in the course of winning the war. Sometimes you may need to end a meal that your teen has not completed because it is getting late and you can't let it drag on. Sometimes you may need to swap out a *fear food*—the foods your teen is too afraid to consume—for something he is more likely to eat. Capitulating in these limited instances does not mean you've failed. Sometimes it's just practical. There will be another opportunity tomorrow.

Watch for these initial signs of progress:

- Weight gain of one to two pounds per week, if this is an identified goal

- Decreased bingeing and purging, even if only because you have made it physically impossible

- Decreased compulsive exercise, even if only because you are preventing it

- Less difficulty at mealtime

- Acceptance of the new routine around eating

- Some increased flexibility in foods eaten

- Faster pace of eating

Research demonstrates that if FBT is going to work, there is usually some visible progress by week 4 (Lock 2016). If you are seeing no signs of progress after a month of structuring meals and interrupting behaviors (as described in chapters 4 through 6), I strongly encourage you to seek additional help. If you are not working with a therapist, it is time to find one; if you are working with a therapist, it may be time for a higher level of care, more intensive support, or a different approach.

If your teen should be gaining weight and if the weight gain slows or stalls, you must determine why. In some cases, the teen may be burning more calories due to weight already gained. As you learned in chapter 5, calorie needs often increase in a stepwise fashion as weight is gained. If you believe this is the case, you will want to increase intake accordingly. You can increase daily calorie intake each week by an additional 500 to 1,000 calories until your teen is again gaining one to two pounds per week.

However, there are other potential reasons for lack of weight gain, including hypermetabolism (which can be associated with night sweats) or increased eating disorder behaviors. The latter could manifest as purging, overexercising, hiding food, and so on. It is not yet time to back off! The eating disorder may have discovered gaps in your supervision. If you have made it impossible for your teen to purge, he may have started to secretly exercise instead. Or he may have figured out a way to hide or discard food when you are not looking. Even missing a snack or two can make a difference. When one loophole is closed, an eating disorder often expresses itself through another. You may need to review your procedures more closely to shut down these opportunities. Observe your teen more carefully after meals to ensure he is not purging, and increase your level of supervision.

Common Challenges Faced by Parents

Supporting teens in recovery is not an easy job, especially for parents, yet they are uniquely qualified for the role. Parents will face pitfalls and challenges, including their own fears, along the way.

Parental Distress

Many parents are overwhelmed by the process of helping their teen with an eating disorder. Sparring with your teen's eating disorder on top of all the typical responsibilities of parenting can be brutal. You are receiving abuse from the eating disorder while at the same time running yourself ragged with all the grocery shopping and meal preparation. No one else in your life can understand the lengths to which you go to support your teen. No one gets it!

Please engage in self-care. As you are instructed on each airplane flight: put on your own oxygen mask before assisting others. You need to maintain your strength, because this can take many months or even years. Find someone who can relieve you, even if only for a select meal or two per week. Make sure you get rest. Seek additional support via individual therapy or a parents' support group or forum. Support from parents who have been there and know what you are going through can be invaluable. Asking for professional help when you need it may also model healthy behavior for your teen.

> ### Getting Additional Support
>
> You and your family are not alone in fighting an eating disorder. In fact, there are many individuals, groups, and organizations that can provide invaluable support, guidance, and information. See my list of these resources at http://www.newharbinger.com/40439.

Trouble Tolerating a Teen's Distress

Aspects of helping your child with an eating disorder violate deep parental instincts. That's because assisting in recovery means repeatedly requiring your teen to face the very situations that distress her. For many parents, there is nothing harder than watching a teen struggle, and then feeling responsible for her distress. As Tony, a father from New Jersey, shares, "For me as a parent, the hardest part was realizing that in requiring my child to eat, it was *going* to cause discomfort and hysteria. There was *no* way around it. There was no 'we will try again later,' because with every bite missed the eating disorder would get a stronger hold on her." Of course, every parent needs to be practical. There are times to hold the line and times to bend.

Keep your eye on the goal. Your teen's distress is temporary. Once you accept that fact you can channel your energy into loving and supporting your teen rather than trying to make him feel better. This also models for your teen that negative emotions can be faced and tolerated. We will discuss coping strategies later in this chapter.

Fear That You Will Ruin Your Teen's Spirit

Many parents are concerned that requiring their teen to eat or limiting their teen's independence will cause permanent harm. Parents often worry that taking control of their teen's recovery will make the eating disorder worse or stunt their teen's development.

Let me be clear: there is no evidence that prioritizing recovery and causing temporary distress to your teen will dampen his spirit or cause permanent damage. What will harm him is the physical and emotional damage wrought by an unchecked eating disorder.

Fear That You Will Destroy Your Relationship with Your Teen

Parents also commonly worry that the steps they must take to fight the eating disorder—such as intrusively supervising them after meals—will undermine their relationship with their teen.

Once again: there is no evidence that parent-supported treatment permanently harms the parent–teen relationship. I suspect that more relationships are permanently damaged when teens and young adults remain chronically ill. The limited research indicates that parental inclusion ultimately strengthens rather than harms the parent–child relationship (Parks, Anderson, and Cusack 2016; Wallis et al. 2017). Ultimately, accounts from those teens and young adults who have recovered with the help of parental support tend to be positive.

However, you should not expect this right away. Only when they are fully recovered and have some distance from the illness are teens and young adults likely to appreciate how much their parents have loved and supported them through the hardest of times.

Fear That Taking Away Favorite Activities Will Make Your Teen More Depressed

In the process of helping your teen, you may have to reduce or end her participation in a favorite sport or other activity. In this situation, many parents worry that the loss of the activity will cause depression.

I will not sugarcoat this: it can. However, this is no reason to allow your teen to participate in a sport that may be detrimental to his health. I have worked with many families whose teen had to sacrifice a favorite sport in favor of recovery. This is painful for all involved. Keep in mind that it is the eating disorder that is the villain here. Allowing your teen to participate in certain activities may perpetuate an eating disorder, keep him ill, and potentially even kill him.

Teens do recover from their disorder, and when healthy they eventually find other activities that bring them joy. Teens who have had to stop playing a sport have gone on to find new passions in music, art, drama, and other school activities. I have seen it happen!

Fear of Your Teen Gaining Too Much Weight

Parents and professionals alike can fear too much weight gain. As discussed in chapter 3, society can put a lot of pressure on parents and professionals to limit weight gain—making them co-conspirators with the eating disorder.

This concern is misplaced. As we saw in chapter 3, return to a healthy weight based on a teen's unique growth curve appears to be a requirement for full brain recovery. You may fear that the eating disorder will get stronger if you push your teen's weight above her phobic threshold. In actuality, this will help her learn that nothing bad happens above that weight. This is another opportunity to embrace and accept your own distress.

Lily, from Pennsylvania, notes this about her daughter:

She is fifteen pounds heavier than what we originally thought she would need to weigh. What's interesting? The weight doesn't bother her now, though she thought she was "disgusting and obese" at a weight forty pounds lighter. That was when her thoughts were disordered because her brain was starved—and that is no longer, thankfully, the case.

Expecting or Wanting the Teen to Assume Responsibility Too Early

Another challenge parents face is expecting or wanting their teen to take over responsibility for recovery too soon. Once things improve a little and parents start to tire, they long for their teen to show their own initiative in tackling the disorder.

But consider: if putting teens in charge of their own recovery worked, there would not be a need for FBT. Remember that most teens are incapable of recovering individually and are unprepared to manage their own meals until parents have systematically moved them through all the steps of eating independence, they have demonstrated signs of readiness to prevent eating disorder behaviors, and they have practiced recovery behaviors on their own.

Fear of Stopping Midway

We've finally reached *my* biggest fear: parents becoming complacent and stopping before recovery is 100 percent complete. This is my worst fear because once teens improve a little and are no longer sick enough to be mandated to treatment, they may return to their normal lives but remain unwell. When things become a little easier, the vigilance of parents relaxes and they may:

- Stop requiring their child to attend treatment sessions

- Not push for full weight gain

- Fail to eradicate all eating disorder behaviors

- Stop short of pushing through all fear foods

- Transition control back to the teen prematurely

The point at which teens are no longer at risk for hospitalization is the point at which they are more likely to fall through the cracks of the health care system. In these situations they are prone to becoming chronically ill. In one study predating FBT, more than two-thirds of patients still suffered from anorexia nervosa after nine years (Eddy et al. 2017). This is far too long to allow someone to suffer.

Believe me: it is important to gradually and systematically proceed through the process of handing back control while still retaining oversight for a period of time. We will discuss how to do this in chapter 9. Please do *not* allow your teen to drop out of treatment, stop all oversight, or prematurely hand back complete control. Your work is not yet done.

Coping Strategies for Parents and Teens

The path to recovery will test the distress tolerance of parents and teens alike. That is because, as discussed above, tolerating uncomfortable events and negative emotions in life is necessary for optimal functioning. No one likes feeling distress, and ignoring or avoiding the feelings will make things worse in the long run. So what do you do? You can learn to confront negative emotions and actively manage them via the use of *coping skills*, strategies that you probably already use to stay calm and focused in difficult situations.

I encourage you to assess your current strategies, consider which of the following techniques you would like to try, and model them for your teen. If your child has a predisposition to anxiety—and many with eating disorders do—giving her tools to help manage anxiety throughout the rest of her life is an important gift.

Here are positive coping skills used successfully by families with whom I have worked:

- **Identifying and labeling feelings.** Naming a feeling is a good first step in attending to your internal experience and accepting negative emotions. When you start to feel yourself becoming upset, you might say to yourself, "I'm feeling angry." Acknowledging and observing the feeling for what it is—a passing state of mind—makes it more manageable.

- **Talking to someone.** Calling a friend or talking to your spouse or someone in a parent support group can be an effective way to release your feelings, gain perspective, and receive empathy from someone who can understand what you are going through.

- **Journaling.** Writing can help you express your feelings and gain clarity about a situation. Even just ten to fifteen minutes of writing once a day, or when you feel upset, can be beneficial.

- **Petting or interacting with a pet.** Pets can be comforting and relieve stress.

- **Relaxation or meditation.** Simple relaxation or meditation exercises can be learned or practiced through several apps and online resources. You can do them individually or as a family.

- **Arts and crafts.** Crafts such as knitting, crocheting, collaging, beading, and coloring can provide both a creative and emotional outlet. The repetitive motion of knitting and similar activities is reported to induce a relaxed state like that associated with meditation and yoga. For the creatively challenged, there are now adult coloring books.

- **Manipulatives such as stress balls or Silly Putty.** Emotions prepare the body for and drive expression through physical actions. Working out physical tension with one's hands can offer a safe release.

- **Music.** Listening to music can intensify and express—or sometimes alter—a negative emotion.

- **Exercise (if indicated).** Any exercise for which you can make time can reduce stress and improve mental well-being. Teens may not be able to tolerate formal exercise but can sometimes take a short walk with parents. Sometimes just a change of scenery or fresh air can do the trick.

- **Taking a bath or shower.** A bath or shower can relax and soothe. However, if your teen is at risk for purging, exercise caution.

- **Meal distraction activities.** As described in chapter 6, these can also provide distraction outside of meals when anxiety is high.

Your teen can learn from you passively by watching you cope—people often learn these skills by observation—and actively through conversation—you can guide him when you notice he seems to be struggling. You want to prevent your teen from resorting to eating disorder behaviors to manage distress.

Managing Weight Gain in the Abdomen

If your teen is gaining weight, it may collect disproportionately at her abdomen. The cruel irony is that patients with anorexia, who are often the most phobic about getting fat, often start recovery by "getting a belly." This poorly understood but well-documented phenomenon (Mayer et al. 2005) is thought to have some protective function for the body after a period of starvation. After about a year at a healthy weight, the fat tends to redistribute more evenly throughout the body (Mayer et al. 2009).

The development of a gut can come as a surprise to most families, but it is a sign of progress in recovery. Your teen—and you—have to learn to tolerate this positive sign. I usually suggest warning the teen of the probability of this physical development, as well as that it will ultimately redistribute according to genetically programmed body type, as long as she remains at a sufficient weight.

Managing Negative Body Image

If your teen has experienced negative body image, it may not have remitted at this point in the recovery process. Body image is usually one of the last symptoms to improve. With full weight restoration and normalization of behaviors, it may improve on its own. Then again, it may not.

Keep in mind that such a large portion of the population—females in particular—has a negative body image that researchers have given it a name: *normative discontent*. In other words, it is considered normal—or certainly not abnormal—to have a negative body image, even for those without an eating disorder. In all likelihood, if you are a human reading this book, you've also struggled with body image, but that does not mean it is pathological.

Therefore, it is unreasonable to expect a teen to suddenly love her body when she recovers from an eating disorder—this would mean she had developed a more positive body image than many people who have never had an eating disorder. Many people lead long, happy, productive lives with a vague discontent about the shape of their thighs. Unfortunately, there is little research on interventions to help teens deal with body image issues and no agreed-upon treatment strategies. Nevertheless, I will suggest some strategies that may help reduce behaviors associated with poor body image.

Tolerating Imperfect Body Image

I believe the most realistic way to deal with body image is through the concept of *distress tolerance*. This means working to accept something that is uncomfortable, rather than fighting against it. If you think about the things in life you wish you had but do not (such as being born into a family of extreme wealth, being tall, or having a natural talent as a musician), you probably notice that you've accepted these perceived shortcomings as something out of your control—and you've made the best of your life without them.

Many people persist in believing that one's natural weight is a characteristic that can be permanently altered. In fact, one's weight is not under one's full control. As we discussed in chapter 3, body weight is largely genetically determined, as are body shape, muscularity, height, and eye color.

The point is: if we expect that a majority of teens will have negative body image, "recovery" includes acceptance that they may never be totally happy with their bodies. It also means learning to tolerate that feeling and to appreciate and accept one's body. Learning to enjoy physical activity as well as rest—and to appreciate the skills, strengths, and capabilities of our bodies—is important for all teens, especially those facing eating disorders.

You can model this attitude by letting your teen know that you understand his body distress, empathizing with the feeling, trying *not* to reassure him that his body type meets arbitrary criteria for weight or muscularity, and not acting too interested.

Activities to Improve Body Image

Here are two strategies that you might try to help your teen improve her body image:

Check your teen's social media feed. Teens are active digitally and may compete for likes on Instagram. They will send each other links to "beautiful" people and share ridiculously posed photos. While this is now considered "normal" social media behavior, it's a good idea to discuss with your teen how seeing this material makes her feel, and how to engage in self-care online. If your teen follows fashion bloggers or celebrities on social media, she may be barraged with images of super-thin (or supermuscular) models and possibly even tips for eating disorder behaviors. You may need to help your child curate a more appropriate feed, unfollowing these people in favor of individuals who promote health and size diversity. Consider searching social media sites under phrases such as "body positive," "nondiet," and "health at every size."

Interrupt body checking. A teen preoccupied with thoughts about weight or shape may engage in behaviors that sustain that preoccupation. One such behavior is *body checking*, the constant observation of one's weight and appearance. One form of this that we've already addressed is compulsive weighing (often many times a day). Body checking can also include studying oneself in the mirror, comparing one's body with others', or measuring specific body parts, such as waist or arm width. Often, people are unaware that they study or check their bodies so frequently. Body checking can become a reflexive habit. Whether conscious or unconscious, it has been implicated in the persistence of eating disorders (Fairburn 2008).

If your teen is engaging in body checking, now is a good time to address it. A simple intervention is redirection of the behavior when you see it or provision of incentives for not checking. You may want to cover mirrors or put in other barriers to inhibit what may have become automatic behavior. For example, if your teen repeatedly checks her thighs, have her wear a long skirt instead of shorts. If your teen lifts his shirt repeatedly to check his abs, have him tuck in his shirt. In chapter 8 we will discuss additional clothing strategies that can also help with body image.

> ## Additional Body Image Activities
>
> In the online materials at http://www.newharbinger.com/40439, I share other activities to address body image. Although outside of the scope of FBT, they may be worthwhile to try with your teen.

Beware of the Extinction Bursts

Let's say that you have been applying the strategies in this book for some time and things are going smoothly. Then, out of the blue, you are faced with a sudden resurgence of eating disorder symptoms, such as increased distress at meals, increased food refusal, or increased purging. This can be confusing and distressing. You might think, "What is going on? Why are things suddenly worse again?" You might even worry that you have lost all the progress you've made.

This is typical of what behavioral psychologists call an *extinction burst*. During the course of eliminating a behavior that is not reinforced, the behavior usually starts to decrease gradually. But just before it disappears completely, the behavior unexpectedly ramps up again. For example, when a child's temper tantrums are no longer getting attention, they actually intensify for a time before they stop appearing. The child is not getting the response he or she wants but thinks, "If I just try harder, my parent will give me what I want." This is the extinction burst.

Some parents have observed this pattern in their teen's recovery. Here's how Alice, a mother from Canada, describes it:

> The "extinction burst" often shows up after a fairly quiet period of eating without too much resistance, gaining weight with diminishing distress, or some other eye-of-the-hurricane-type lulls. You think you have a handle on this illness and then BOOM—behaviors show up with a vengeance. Or maybe just an uptick in behaviors. Sometimes it's a dramatic change, almost a reversion to early refeeding. Sometimes it's more subtle. Sometimes, like with my daughter, it exhibits in behaviors that are not directly related to eating.

The problem is that it is often hard to recognize an extinction burst until it has passed. What is most important to remember is that no recovery from any mental disorder is a straight upward trajectory. All recoveries have fits and starts. When you hit what seems like an increase in symptoms, it is helpful to remember that it is likely a normal part of the recovery process; it doesn't mean that you are doing anything wrong. It's often a time to take a breath, redouble your efforts, and wait it out.

Closing Thoughts

In this chapter, you have learned about the course of recovery and how to determine whether your interventions are having an impact on your teen's eating disorder. You also have learned additional strategies for managing common challenges. In the next chapter, we will address how to increase your teen's flexibility.

CHAPTER 8

Exposure to Build Flexibility

Once your management of meals and other behaviors has built a certain momentum, and you are making progress and handling everyday challenges, it is time to turn your attention to building your teen's flexibility. He may now be able to eat regular meals at home but may not yet be able to eat in other settings. The range of foods he will eat may still be abnormally narrow. His behaviors with respect to clothing, exercise, schedules, and other aspects of daily life may remain uncomfortably rigid. In this chapter you will learn how to develop a plan to increase your teen's flexibility.

Maintain Structure

The structure you have carefully built during the last several months to support your teen has been essential to getting you through the early phases of recovery. Regular eating schedules and consistent expectations for your teen have been the mainstays of the work thus far. In this structured environment, it is easier to begin the process of recovery. Structure makes things predictable and reduces anxiety.

However, life is unpredictable, and your teen must eventually tolerate different and more challenging situations. The focus of this chapter is preparing your teen to handle a range of scenarios, gradually relaxing some of the structure you've built. This will allow your teen to stay in recovery and face successively greater challenges.

Exposure to Different Foods

If your teen has a lot of fear foods, you may not have gotten to this point without reintroducing at least a few of them. But once meals start going more smoothly, some weight has been gained, and binges and purges have been regulated, many parents are reluctant to push further. Why rock the boat when your teen seems to be doing well?

In fact, this is exactly the right time to begin introducing (more) fear foods. It is much easier to introduce these foods before the child is completely weight restored and when parents are still in full charge of meals and the teen does not yet have his independent life back. The logistics of pushing the issue become more challenging when your otherwise healthy teen has regained most of his freedom but won't go to his club meeting for fear of the pizza being served there.

ONLINE ACTIVITY 10: My Teen's Fear Foods

If you need help compiling a list of your teen's fear foods, refer to the online materials for this book at http://www.newharbinger .com/40439. There you will find examples of the most frequently cited fear foods for teens with eating disorders. Your list may be different.

When you introduce fear foods to your teen, you will probably feel increased anxiety and resistance, and your teen will too. You may feel like you are going back a step. This is how exposure works—it is supposed to raise your teen's anxiety. When she avoids these fear foods, she receives a reward: decreased anxiety. This reinforcement perpetuates the fear and avoidance. But to those of us outside the eating disorder, it is clear that eating the feared foods will have no ill effects. In exposure, the teen is required to eat the food: when there are no negative consequences, the anxiety response shows itself to be baseless. With repeated exposure the brain habituates and learns that the food is not harmful (Hildebrandt et al. 2012).

Why Do I Have to Eat Pizza?

I often get this question from teens and even some parents. It's also a common negotiation strategy: teens can be skillful at convincing parents that eating pizza is unnecessary for their recovery. Given the frequency with which this issue arises, I share my thoughts here.

There are a few foods that are ubiquitous, at least in the United States. Pizza is one of them. Think about how many events you have attended where the primary food was pizza. Whether it's a late-night dorm study session or a birthday party for a person of any age, it is hard to avoid events with pizza. It's also one of the most common fear foods.

If you want your teen to be able to live a full life, you must reckon with this food. You can approach it gradually—many teens seem to find it easier to start with a "healthier" homemade pizza or a less greasy pizza from a gourmet restaurant. However, I believe your teen is not safe in the world until he can eat a slice or two of Domino's, grease and all.

I also think it is important to prepare your teen to eat the foods she is likely to eat with peers. When you start to give your teen greater independence around food, she is likely to eat some meals with peers. Think about which foods are likely to be encountered in these situations. Besides pizza, the usual suspects include pancakes and bagels (often served for breakfast after sleepovers), Starbucks flavored coffee drinks, popcorn, and cheeseburgers. It is worth prioritizing a few of these specific foods on your exposure plan.

Regarding desserts, registered dietitian nutritionist Katie Grubiak's philosophy is that dessert should be offered every night until it is no longer resisted. If your teen continues to protest dessert, it is too early to back off.

Fear Foods

It's now time to build an exposure hierarchy based on your prior work listing the foods your teen used to eat (Online Activity 7). Please pull out that list (or complete it now). Review the items and rank them from easiest to hardest in terms of what you think your child will agree to eating. Consider which foods are similar to foods in your teen's current diet. For example, if she is already eating toast for breakfast, you might introduce English muffins. Foods she gave up more recently are the foods you may want to reintroduce sooner. You should add to the list foods on which she binges. Your goal is to help your teen incorporate common serving sizes of these foods into her regular meals or snacks.

You can try breaking down fear foods into smaller steps. For example, when working on pasta you can start with a small side serving or a pasta salad with vegetables as a first step. Over time, you might next serve pasta as a main dish with a marinara sauce, eventually working up to a main course of pasta with a richer cream or pesto sauce.

Exposure works through repetition over a stretch of time (not necessarily all in a row): each food on your list should be revisited several times until the thought of eating it no longer causes extreme anxiety.

ONLINE ACTIVITY 11: Fear Foods Exposure

Now that you have thought about which foods your teen fears, you can list them in the order you plan to reintroduce them to her diet. Visit http://www.newharbinger.com/40439 for detailed instructions on planning exposure. Use this in conjunction with the Exposure Record included in the online materials.

Whenever you notice your teen balking at eating something, expressing anxiety about a food, or refusing a food—whether or not it is on this list—you don't need to make a big deal about it. Just make a mental note and add that food to the list of fear foods so that you can remember to incorporate it in your exposures.

Many parents have become so conditioned by the eating disorder that they subconsciously structure family meals around foods they know their teen will eat. This will not help you conquer the eating disorder. By serving the fear foods again to the rest of the family, you can set the stage for your teen to eat them. The teen may refuse the first few exposures, but with repeated introductions and observation of other family members eating these foods, his willingness to try will increase. In some cases, he may even ask to eat the food.

Eating Outside the Home

Many parents are surprised to find that their teen in early recovery has difficulty eating in different contexts. While a day at Disneyland, dinner at Grandma's house, or a quick lunch while running errands may be part of a "normal" family life for most, these outings can be challenging with an inflexible teen in recovery.

Once meals at home are proceeding smoothly, you can start to eat with your teen in different settings, such as restaurants, school, or friends' houses. This will allow you to eventually resume your normal family life and to travel. If your child has not yet practiced eating outside the home, he is not ready for travel or even a day at an amusement park. But he will get there—in time.

Handling Travel

Eating outside the home may at some point involve travel. Visit http://www.newharbinger.com/40439 for tips on traveling with a teen with an eating disorder.

Just as with exposure to fear foods, it is good to proceed with exposure to different food settings gradually and thoughtfully. Many teens have an easier time at restaurants that are more familiar, "healthier," or that prepare the food in front of the customer.

ONLINE ACTIVITY 12: Restaurant Exposure

To help you create a plan to gradually broaden the settings in which your child is able to eat safely, visit http://www.newharbinger.com/40439. There you'll find instructions for introducing different contexts as well as space to list the places you'd like to visit. You will use this in conjunction with the Exposure Record included in the online materials.

If it used to be common to eat at a grandparent's house or have a picnic lunch after church, plan a strategy to resume these meals. In these informal settings, I suggest that parents nonchalantly, and without any public discussion, make a plate for their teen just as they would at home. It is usually a good idea to prepare your teen for such occasions: "We're going to have dinner at Grandma's house. I'll make a plate for you just like I do at home and you'll be expected to eat it."

If these first few forays into new contexts do not go well, remember: this is not failure. It is simply feedback that the setting was too much for your teen at this time. You can review whether there was anything specific you would do differently the next time. Adjust your plan and wait a few weeks before trying again. If this attempt goes successfully, you can introduce your teen to the next setting challenge.

Here is how Veronica, from New York, describes her daughter's restaurant challenge:

> We took our daughter to a burger restaurant that we used to go to every summer. She was miserable, hiding in the corner of the booth, unable to even look up at us. She had loved these burgers pre-eating disorder. I dangled the "if you can't eat with us, I'm afraid to let you try eating with your friends" veiled threat and, all of a sudden, she gobbled it down. It was sort of repulsive and sad—she couldn't enjoy it. But she did it and was quietly distressed for a long while after. She didn't cry and stomp and pull it apart and pace around the restaurant like she has in the past on these nights.
>
> Later, she came down to watch TV with us and admitted she felt better. It really was a big change from how she's handled it in the past. It wasn't pretty or enjoyable, but it was better.
>
> I really felt like we were literally chipping away at the eating disorder.

Exposure to Different Clothing

Many teens have discomfort with clothing. Body image concerns related to an eating disorder can pile additional woes on top of the usual teenage angst. In addition, your child might outgrow clothes as he recovers weight. Approaching clothing with compassion is important.

For teens who have gained weight, it is best for parents to remove undersize clothing (preferably making it disappear entirely through donation or the like) without comment and replace it with clothing that fits. Some parents try to reduce their teen's anxiety over weight gain by routinely taking the sizing labels out of the new clothes they provide.

Some teens develop avoidant behaviors regarding clothing. They may steer clear of clothing that is fitted, revealing, or even season-appropriate. Or they may repeatedly wear a single clothing item in much the same way some children stick with safe foods.

If your teen refuses to wear shorts, sleeveless shirts, or bathing suits—or to vary her clothes—you can use the same exposure strategy used with fear foods or different eating contexts: pick a starting point and ascend the ladder gradually. For example, if your teen has been hiding in baggy sweatpants, a bathing suit may be several steps away; a more realistic first step is requiring a fitted pair of jeans. You may need to break this exposure down further by having her practice wearing jeans first in the house, then on an errand, and eventually to school.

Angelica, from Nevada, describes a clothing intervention with her daughter:

> We had a difficult time with clothes restriction after weight restoration. We were down to one pair of black sweatpants for months and months. For my daughter, the anxiety over food seemed to morph to fear over clothes. We did clothing exposure. We went gradually (tried wearing something different for one hour on the weekend, then for the afternoon, then outside, etc.). My daughter needed a lot of validation around the clothes. She felt awful that she wore the same thing every day, but she was too frightened to wear anything else. I had to tell her over and over that I understood it was anxiety, that it was okay, that we would sort it out, that she was brave, and so on.

ONLINE ACTIVITY 13: Clothing Exposure

To help you create a plan for gradually broadening the outfits your teen feels comfortable wearing, visit http://www.newharbinger .com/40439. There you will find instructions for getting your child to vary his wardrobe and in what order. You will use this worksheet in conjunction with the Exposure Record included in the online materials.

Promoting Appropriate Exercise

It's important to distinguish between exercise that is aimed at altering shape and weight and exercise that is meant to provide joy or general health benefits. Eating disorders push individuals to change their bodies by driving them to perform calisthenics, exercise frequently and intensely, and feel anxious if they cannot exercise. Teens free of eating disorders typically do not desire to engage in strength training, calis-thenics, or using workout machines beyond what is suggested for spe-cific sports training; they can also better tolerate not being able to exercise.

Keep in mind that if your teen struggles with compulsive exercise, has medical restrictions against exercise, or remains underweight, then it will be prudent for you to continue to prohibit exercise.

If your teen does not have these issues, you may want to start to think about allowing him to engage in appropriate and monitored movement. However, if exercise contributed to the development of the eating disorder, you will not want your teen to abruptly resume activity at the pre-recovery level. Instead, redirect him toward activities that are safer and more appropriate, given the risk of exercise-driven relapse.

The very word "exercise" may bring up ideas of compensating for consumed calories. On the other hand, "movement" can describe a broader allowance of the fun activities of which the body is capable.

This simple reframing can help you identify the types of activities you want your teen in recovery to pursue.

I suggest age-appropriate, noncompetitive, and social activities, such as hiking, noncompetitive dancing, yoga, walking, rock climbing, bike riding, skateboarding, or surfing. It is a good idea to start out slowly, practicing a new activity once or twice per week for no more than a half hour. You will want to make sure this does not impact weight or impede weight gain before increasing the amount of exercise. Sometimes you need to add more food to compensate for the additional calories burned by the activity.

James, a father from Michigan says:

> My daughter, who was diagnosed with anorexia at age ten, begged for three years to run track. We said, "No. Never. No." When she was sixteen, I asked her if she was still interested in track. She looked at me like I was nuts and said, "I hate running. That wasn't me, Dad—it was the eating disorder."

Think about your teen's position on the exercise spectrum. Taking into consideration recommendations from any treating professionals, ponder how you can help your teen find balance in exercise and what activities you might encourage.

Closing Thoughts

In this chapter, you have learned strategies to increase your teen's flexibility in the realms of food, clothing, and exercise. In the next chapter, we will discuss strategies to increase your teen's independence around eating.

CHAPTER 9

Handing Back Control and Working Toward Independence

After working through weight restoration, interruption of behaviors, and increasing flexibility, you have made tremendous progress. At this point, your teen may look like Sam. Sam's parents have successfully helped him to restore weight and to stop bingeing, purging, and exercising. He eats a variety of foods and consumes all his meals, including school lunches, under parental supervision. He stays in the family room after school while he does his homework so his parents can ensure he is not exercising. Sam still engages in some body checking and a bit of compulsive body movement while seated. He is monitored when he goes to the bathroom. Sam's bedroom door always remains open. He has not been able to socialize with friends. He is in remission from symptoms, but how should his parents work on increasing his independence and restoring him to normal teenage life?

Helping your teen to maintain a stable weight and refrain from eating disorder behaviors is an accomplishment. However, your teen is likely not yet ready for independent eating. In this chapter, you'll discover how you can slowly but systematically remove the scaffolding you built earlier to support your teen's recovery and move him toward full independent eating and maintenance of his own recovery.

Knowing When to Hand Back Control

The FBT manual for anorexia nervosa specifies three criteria for handing back control:

1. The teen is at or near a healthy weight.

2. Meals are going more smoothly.

3. Parents feel confident in their ability to help their child.

The FBT manual for bulimia nervosa adds a fourth criterion:

4. Other eating disorder behaviors, such as bingeing, purging, and excessive exercise, are in remission.

If you are at this point, congratulations on your progress toward restoring your child's health! You've worked hard to save your teen's life. It can be scary to think about giving back control. This is a natural response, after all you've been through.

Looking at the eating independence continuum (Online Activity 3), review where on the continuum your teen is now. She may have naturally moved a little farther along to the right. Some parents intuitively start to allow their teen a little independence during the course of treatment. If you haven't, that's okay. That's what we're going to work on now. Review where your child needs to go; as discussed in chapter 3, this is determined by age.

Let's hear some parents describe what this middle murky phase of handing back control looked like at various points for their teens.

He can select and get his own snack out of the cupboard when instructed at snack time.

Our daughter can go on sleepovers, eat snacks with friends, and occasionally choose her snack, but we still supervise all meals.

She eats lunch with friends at school, but that is really the only meal she eats unsupervised at this time. She can eat with friends, but I still tell her what to get when she goes out with them. We still supervise breakfast, after-school snack, and dinner.

He no longer needs to use the bathroom after meals, or, if he does, he'll say, "Hey, I'm off to the bathroom, back in a minute," and leave the door ajar when he goes in. It is now becoming his own form of supervision.

I supervise him making his own breakfast; then I help plan his lunch, which he eats at school with friends. He serves himself at dinner.

When we were confident that school lunch could be managed independently again, we put a safety net in place. No bathroom use after lunch, and lunch has to be eaten with certain people (good friends) and in a certain place. This structure is working well. He is also aware that the consequences will be full supervision or no school. This gives him huge motivation.

When he started to go back to sleepovers, I would brief the parent and make a plan with my son about how it would be handled.

She selects about 90 percent of her food on her own. We supervise only breakfast and dinner now, and she generally texts photos of lunch and snacks that she eats on her own. She serves herself adequate amounts at family meals. She continues to eat "extra" things when she feels like it.

Teaching Your Child to Ride a Bike

During the past several months, you have been scrutinizing your teen. You know when he has eaten insufficiently, which foods he needs to eat to be well, and the timing of meals and portion sizes that supply him enough energy and keep him from bingeing. You know when your teen is overexercising, when he is at risk for purging, and when he is struggling. You have much valuable information about your teen. He may not yet comprehend this information and may still have little insight or motivation to recover. That is normal and okay. You will want to eventually transfer this hard-learned knowledge to your teen. You will be teaching him recovery skills.

There is no way to predict precisely how your teen will handle more eating independence. It is mostly trial and error. Setbacks are likely. I liken this phase to teaching a child to ride a bike. When you taught your child to ride a bike, it likely went like this: you put your kid on the bike seat, held the bike steady, and ran alongside the bike as it started moving. Once she had some momentum, you let go but ran alongside her. Inevitably, she fell off, but from your position nearby you caught her before she got badly hurt. You steadied her on the bike seat again and repeated the routine until your child got on, started pedaling, and rode entirely on her own.

So it is with handing back eating independence. You must assign your teen simple recovery tasks and let go for a bit to see if she teeters. Letting go is frightening. You might see that your child is unsteady and that you need to hold on a little longer or a lot longer. Or she might be able to do this independently. More likely it's somewhere in the middle. She can go for a time before crashing, but you must anticipate these mishaps, intervene before they grow into relapses, get her back on track, and repeat as necessary.

The only way to know whether your teen is ready to take on a specific task is to test it. You can give your teen small opportunities to "prove" that she can do it. Run an experiment and see how it goes. Just go slowly.

Breaking Independence Into Steps

When a family is ready to return some independence to the teen, I usually suggest introducing one new degree of responsibility at a time and going slowly. For example, you might have your teen make a plate at dinner, portioning the different elements of the meal as he thinks you would. The key rule in this activity is that your child must accept being corrected if you think he under-portioned a food. If your teen gets upset when corrected, then he is not ready to handle that task independently.

You might be wondering, "Should we let our teen choose her snacks? Or should we let her pack her own lunch and eat on her own?" There is tremendous ambiguity, and there are many decisions to make. Every family has its own strategies and solutions, and there is no one right way to do things. And every teen has a different level of motivation and readiness for taking back control. It can be hard to distinguish a desire for independence from the demands of the eating disorder; some teens plead to spend time with friends while others show little motivation and need more encouragement. In some cases, you can offer an incentive for a step toward independence if the independence itself is not inherently rewarding. Do not expect smooth sailing in this phase. And do not rush it.

Here are some ways to hand back control. This list is not comprehensive, and I encourage you to identify situations based on your own family's routines and customs.

- Let her decide between two equivalent options for a snack.

- Let him choose among multiple options for a snack.

- Have her choose a snack and show it to you.

- Allow him to make a choice between two equivalent alternatives for an element of the meal (for example, pasta or rice).

- Permit her to portion her own plate, which you check and correct, if necessary.

- Have him prepare and pack his own school lunch, which you check and correct, if necessary.

- Allow her to take a packed lunch to school, with a responsible party checking whether it has been eaten.

- Let him make his own breakfast or lunch on the weekend as you watch.

- Permit her to eat at a friend's house, with a report back from the friend's parent.

- Permit him to sleep over at a friend's house and eat a meal or two there, with confirmation of eating by the friend's parent.

- Allow her to go out to eat with a friend at a place you've previously eaten together.

- Permit him to eat meals out with friends.

- Let her eat a meal alone at home while FaceTiming with you.

- Allow him to eat a meal at home when you are out and have him report back to you.

- Ask her to help cook dinner.

- Ask him to plan a meal.

Handing back control of school lunches is a reasonable early step toward autonomy. However, I suggest you break this step down further: start with one day of independence a week, or move to partial supervision before abandoning supervision entirely.

If any steps result in bargaining, questioning, or undue anxiety—or you can tell that your teen's internal calorie counter is frantically calculating and comparing to choose the leanest option—then you can matter-of-factly, not punitively, say, "I don't think you're ready for this yet. We'll try again later."

Remember that cognitive recovery is impossible if eating disorder behaviors continue. If your teen cannot complete a specific task without engaging in eating disorder behaviors (for example, if he cannot go out to eat with friends without restricting, serve himself dessert, or stop himself from exercising), you must continue to supervise, correct, and redirect him to recovery behaviors.

You want to scrutinize—and weigh—your teen as you make these first few forays into independence. If your teen's weight drops, she purges, or you notice any exacerbation of behavior, it is best to take a step back. Two steps forward and one step back is a common theme of this phase. Your teen's inability to handle a specific situation at this time is feedback for you—she is not yet ready for that step—not an indication of failure. You simply reclaim control and try again in a few weeks or a few months. It's essential that parents feel empowered to fight the eating disorder, because they must always be ready to step back in if needed.

Some teens may need parents to remain in complete charge for years. Some teens clearly want continued guidance and supervision; they may have insight into their own vulnerability and desire a safety net. I tend to respect that and tell parents there is no need to rush recovery. But I assure you that I have heard of no teens who were unable to eventually gain more independence.

Another challenge during this phase may be that your teen *looks* well. Those in your life who don't understand eating disorders may assume your teen is now healthy. However, you must remain vigilant and continue supervising your child.

If your teen does show mastery of a specific step, then you can move on to a more challenging step. Go slow and be patient.

Relaxing Oversight Over Other Behaviors

After a period of regular balanced eating and abstention from exercise, bingeing, and purging, the urges to engage in these activities often subside. Concurrently, your teen's ability to resist them should strengthen.

If you have been supervising your teen to prevent these behaviors, it is time to consider loosening these controls. Your teen may be able to assume some responsibility for independently engaging in distraction activities after meals and resisting urges when they arise.

You can think about breaking this phase into smaller steps as well, such as:

- Letting your teen return to sleeping in his room, but continuing to monitor for the sounds of exercise

- Permitting your teen to go to the bathroom after meals, but having her take the initiative to let you know and to keep the door cracked open

- Decreasing your post-meal monitoring from sixty minutes to thirty

- Stopping the supervision of lower-risk meals altogether

- Allowing your teen to shower with the bathroom door shut

- Allowing your teen to do homework in another room

Take caution when concurrently relaxing oversight in multiple areas, which may make it difficult to identify specific backsliding behaviors. For example, if you allow lunches alone at school *and* a return to sleeping in his own room, when he loses four pounds you won't know whether the weight loss is due to skipped lunches or exercising at night.

Teaching Portions

I find that many parents don't appreciate the importance of teaching portioning skills to teens with eating disorders. Many individuals with eating disorders suffer from perceptual distortions: they accurately judge neither food nor their own body size (Milos et al. 2013). They are unprepared for *intuitive eating*—a person's reliance on his or her own internal cues to regulate eating. You and your children who did not contract eating disorders may be able to make a plate and know how much to eat—but this skill does not come naturally for a teen with an eating disorder.

Most people without eating disorders are used to deciding how to portion their food based on visualizing it on their plate. This is healthier than relying on calorie counts and more convenient than measuring food—so much so that the USDA has actually replaced its old nutrition guide, the food pyramid, with the "MyPlate" framework. It is desirable to teach individuals with eating disorders to portion their food this way. Over time and with repetition, you want your teen to learn visually what quantity of food is right for him. Letting your teen portion his plate with corrections until he can do it the same way you have been is an essential way to build this skill. Practice in different settings, working your way up to buffets, which tend to be the most challenging setting.

Scheduled Eating

One of the goals for recovery is the return to intuitive eating. We know that the cues of hunger and satiety become unreliable when an individual has an eating disorder. Recovery of internal hunger cues can be slow. It does not usually occur until many months after weight recovery and cessation of eating disorder behaviors. Until these cues return, your teen may need to rely on external rules, such as the structure and guidelines you have developed about how much and when to eat to support her health.

This doesn't mean you should not transfer any control back to your teen. It just means that she needs to be able to follow the guidelines without straying. While most individuals do recover intuitive eating skills eventually, some may always need greater structure then pure reliance on intuitive eating—and that is okay! Do not expect your teen to initiate eating or to eat spontaneously during this phase.

Reengaging with the Outside World

It is also during this phase when your teen, now more stable, can broaden his reengagement with the outside world. Eating disorders typically disrupt normal teen activities and can pull teens off their normal developmental trajectory. Now you want to help your teen reengage in activities and with peers.

This reengagement goes hand in hand with gradually letting your teen have more meals unsupervised. For example, it is a good idea to let your teen start with a single meal away from you. If that seems to be going well, she could be allowed to go on sleepovers, go away for the weekend on a school trip, or the like. If weight is not lost and behaviors don't change, the teen might be permitted to go on a longer one-week trip.

Many people with eating disorders tend to evaluate their self-worth based largely on their shape and weight, and their ability to control them (Fairburn 2008). Over time, other interests have taken a back seat. But one way to reduce this overevaluation of shape and weight, and the ability to control them, is to enrich other areas of their lives. Putting more time and energy into other meaningful activities—such as hobbies, volunteering, social activities, family, and their community—can reduce teens' overreliance on shape and weight as a source of self-esteem. They become more well-rounded individuals. Ultimately, a life worth living can be a strong motivation to maintain recovery.

Practice Increases Success

Remember when we discussed the transition from more to less structure in chapter 8? Keep this in mind as you think about steps toward independence. As you give your teen more freedom, he will be exposed to a broader range of settings in which he hasn't yet practiced recovery skills. You can help by anticipating and simulating these settings for him.

For example, when your teen can eat pancakes at home with you, you can be more confident that she can sleep at a friend's house and eat pancakes there for breakfast. Practice eating a snack at the movies with your teen before you expect her to do the same with friends. Some parents also choose to add additional accountability, such as having their teen send photos of the food they order while out with friends, as an interim step.

Although holidays and special occasions are challenging for most people in recovery, they offer special practice opportunities. On Halloween, for example, most parents find that their child with eating disorders will happily avoid all candy. However, I think this provides an opportunity. Since it is "normal" for teens without eating disorders to eat Halloween candy, I usually encourage parents to incorporate some candy into their teen's snacks that week.

Other holidays provide the opportunity to practice on foods that your teen may not have eaten recently. Preparation is key. Regardless of where exactly your teen is in recovery, you may want to discuss with him ahead of time how you plan to handle the meal. In chapter 8, you learned some strategies for eating at relatives' houses. You can apply the same strategies to holidays. Remember: your teen's anxiety is likely heightened in unfamiliar settings and around foods she has not eaten in a while.

Continue to Build Flexibility

In this phase, you also want to continue to build flexibility. *Fear learning* generalizes—that is, when the brain becomes fearful of something, it automatically becomes fearful of other similar things. This is protective. If our ancient ancestors became ill from eating poisonous berries, they may have reflexively learned to avoid all types of berries. However, fear *unlearning* does not generalize. Our ancestors would have had to individually try out each type of berry to overcome their fear.

The same thing applies to kids with eating disorders. Fearful kids often must be exposed to each variation of food several times. Parents are usually surprised that exposure to one kind of deli turkey doesn't necessarily generalize to a different cut or brand of turkey, or to turkey meatloaf or turkey burgers. Your teen may need exposure to many different variations of the same thing. It's also possible that foods you haven't served in a while can suddenly instigate fear when they are reintroduced. This is one reason it is so important to make sure your teen's flexibility is increasing and that you keep rotating food selections.

Some teens also struggle when parents combine more foods (that is, add a third element to dishes once the child can handle two, such as pancakes with both syrup and bananas instead of pancakes with just syrup), vary quantities, or vary the family's meal schedule. Therefore, these are good things to practice! One challenge might be switching up the schedule and having brunch on a weekend day, which disrupts the timing of other meals and often increases anxiety. Other flexibility challenges might be serving breakfast foods for dinner, serving pizza as a snack, or stopping for an impromptu snack when you pass an ice cream parlor on the way home from an activity.

Flexibility Test

When working with families, I encourage the "Green Eggs and Ham" test: the ultimate goal is for your child to be able to eat in a boat, with a goat, in the rain, on a train…in a word: anywhere. This will allow your teen the freedom to live the fullest life, with the knowledge that she can travel and appropriately nourish herself while protecting against her genetic vulnerability.

Don't Rush It

Take your time as you hand back control. Parents of older teens often feel pressure to hand back control so that their teen may go to college as scheduled. However, I caution against this. Delaying college, if necessary, is a better course of action than rushing. It is safer to take your time.

It is also important to recognize that the amount of time needed for this phase can vary widely. While the FBT manual indicates that this phase can be negotiated in a matter of months, not every family will be able to do so. Some families should keep the parents in charge for much longer, even an additional year or two, before handing back control.

Closing Thoughts

In this chapter we have discussed how you can return control over eating and other behaviors to your teen in a systematic way. This process can be challenging. Sometimes you have to take a step back before moving forward again. So take it slow. As your teen starts to gain independence, he will start to get his life back. You will begin to see the light at the end of the tunnel. In the final chapter I will talk about recovery and relapse prevention.

CHAPTER 10

Recovery and Relapse Prevention

If you've made it this far, you should feel proud of all you've done to help your teen. I know it hasn't been easy. You are probably anxious to have your child live freely. However, I must caution you that recovery can be fragile if it's not watched closely. You are not yet out of the woods. Relapse rates for eating disorders are high even after successful treatment. You must remain vigilant. In this chapter, you'll learn what recovery can look like and how to put relapse prevention strategies in place.

What Does Recovery Look Like?

Ellen, a mother in Kansas, describes her teen's recovery:

> She is completely and totally eating on her own. We often have family meals together, but a lot of the time she is on her own. She eats with complete freedom and gusto. She loves to cook and finds recipes—complete with cream and butter and cheese. She is most definitely tuned in to other people and eating. She voices concerns about other people she knows—and speaks up. She gained about four pounds in the past year, completely intuitively and naturally, like a normal teenager.
>
> She is strong and funny and witty, and every single day I am amazed by her. This kid nearly died. She was a very, very sick little kid. It took 6,000-plus calories a day for years. The battles were endless but we won the war! We have come so far in the last six years.

Researchers have yet to totally agree upon a definition of eating disorder recovery. However, there is agreement that recovery is more nuanced than mere weight restoration or the cessation of behaviors. As discussed in chapter 7, research has covered three main aspects of recovery: remission of symptoms, weight recovery, and psychological recovery. Here I will expand on them and add a fourth: recovery of hunger cues.

Remission of Eating Disorder Behaviors

Remission means that the teen is not restricting, bingeing, purging, using laxatives, or overexercising. It also means he can eat independently and flexibly in a variety of settings. Your teen should be freely eating all the same foods he used to eat about two years before there were any signs of an eating disorder and not restricting his diet in any way. He does not appear obsessive about exercise, does not use it to counteract the effects of eating or to control body shape, and can tolerate days off from exercise.

Weight (and Physical) Recovery

Your teen's weight has been restored. Her body has recovered physically and she has healthy body functions, including normal periods, a healthy heart, and stable blood pressure. Hormonal and metabolic function have returned to normal. She has recovered from any prior symptoms of malnutrition (except perhaps residual bone weakness, which can be permanent) and is back to the health she enjoyed before the eating disorder.

Psychological Recovery

Psychological recovery is usually assessed by tests measuring eating disorder thoughts and other symptoms, such as anxiety and depression. In the real world, parents talk about an improved "state" that is highly noticeable. Psychological recovery includes both emotional and cognitive recovery, which may occur concurrently or at different times.

Emotional Recovery

Parents notice an improvement in mood, a renewed interest in activities other than dieting and exercise, and a return to behaviors such as laughing and singing. Teens can emotionally tolerate situations that might provoke some anxiety, along with situations that they previously avoided when more ill, such as wearing a variety of clothing, eating a range of foods, eating dessert, and skipping exercise.

Cognitive Recovery

In recovery, there will be decreased frequency and intensity of eating disorder thoughts, urges to restrict, urges to purge, and so on. When these thoughts do still occasionally occur, your teen can tolerate them without temptation to act on them. In recovery, your teen is likely to experience negative body image thoughts. In fact, some degree of these thoughts may remain forever. People without eating disorders have negative body image thoughts on a regular basis; the difference is that the people who do not have eating disorders do not act on them.

Recovery of Hunger Cues

Internal cues of hunger and fullness, and the ability to respond to them, are typically disrupted when teens have eating disorders. In recovery, the ability to recognize and respond to signals of hunger and fullness normalizes. Some early signs of recovery of internal cues include behaviors such as your teen asking when dinner will be ready. She may ask for more food, take food autonomously, or spontaneously eat outside of a scheduled meal or snack. A teen in recovery saying she is hungry is usually music to parents' ears.

Examples of Recovery

Let's look at how some parents describe recovery in their teens:

Recovery was the first time she said she was hungry! It was well into refeeding—perhaps close to a year. A very joyful day for me.

It was two years or so after my daughter's diagnosis and we were at brunch. My daughter went to the buffet and got a plate of food and, shortly after eating it, exclaimed that she just had to go back to the buffet because the biscuits were so great that she wanted another. It was magical to hear my daughter talk about how great something tasted and then go back for seconds. I knew then that she was fully in recovery.

For us, the light returning to her eyes and flashes of her normal, dry, sarcastic, and frequent witty banter assured us that we were on the right path to freeing her from the clutches of anorexia.

He is fully social, he does not need to check what restaurant he is going to in advance, and he is enjoying food and its social aspect again without fear. He looks like any other teenager: he is happy to come to the table for all meals and will look for his meals when he is hungry.

Relapse Prevention

While recovery certainly occurs over time for most people with eating disorders, the flip side is that eating disorders tend to be chronic illnesses—and relapses are common. Your teen will retain some of the predisposing factors that contributed to her eating disorder, whether that is a genetic vulnerability, a predisposition to anxiety or perfectionistic traits, a certain temperament, brain chemistry that puts her at risk for response to an energy imbalance, or a combination of these factors. These same factors also put her at risk for reoccurrences.

Relapse prevention research teaches us to plan for relapses and to catch lapses—slips that fall short of full relapses—before they become serious. I believe in observing your teen for several years after full recovery and through any times of transition. This could be an uncomfortable situation as he enters adulthood, but it's important to not call off the fight just because the age of majority has been reached. Many young adults in recovery continue to need and benefit from their parents' ongoing support and vigilance.

Watch for Risky Situations

Here are five situations that may increase the risk for relapse: life transitions, increasing time away from home, peer influences, stressful events, and sudden changes in eating or exercise habits.

Life transitions. Times of transition are common triggers for relapse. Parents report that a fair number of teens who were successfully treated during adolescence relapsed in college. College, in addition to often being the first period when your young adult will be away from you for months at a time, brings numerous other challenges. Other transitions and life events include getting married, moving to a new city, and having a baby.

Transitioning to College

Because transitioning to college can be challenging on multiple levels, it's important to take an honest look at what being on his or her own will mean for your teen. Refer to http://www.newharbinger. com/40439 for a college-readiness checklist, tips for preparing your teen for college, and more.

Increasing time away from home. I believe that any time your teen (or young adult) takes a big step toward increased independence is a time for increased vigilance. Going away on a school trip or to summer camp, or even starting to drive and going out for more meals with friends, can be examples. Do not assume that your teen, who has maintained a healthy weight and healthy behaviors while eating most meals with you, can automatically replicate that behavior in other contexts. Whenever he eventually moves out, you want to be watchful—even if he was treated at age twelve and the disorder is six years in the rearview mirror.

Peer influences. The challenge of peers can potentially be triggering. Dieting by friends—which can increase around prom, around spring break trips, or for no apparent reason at all—should be watched.

Stressful events. Watch your teen more carefully around times of stress. These can range from exam periods and the college application process to family illnesses and relationship breakups. Remember that many who are prone to eating disorders may feel calmer when they do not eat, or they may use food to self-soothe. One teen with bulimia nervosa who was in partial recovery told me that her anxiety was so high the night she expected her college acceptance letter that it was almost impossible to eat.

Sudden change in eating or exercise habits. Plan carefully in any situation that may cause your teen to have an energy imbalance or a legitimate reason to eat less or become more active. Such situations may include:

- Dental surgery, such as wisdom teeth extraction or getting braces

- Illness—teens with eating disorders often think being ill is an excuse to not eat; it is not!

- Religious fasts

- Changes in schedule

- Growth spurts

- Increased sports participation

Approach these potentially risky situations with caution. Weigh your teen before and after these events, and observe carefully. If her weight goes down, or you observe any increased anxiety or eating disorder behaviors afterward, be prepared to reassume control for a brief time. It is far better to be overly cautious than to risk a relapse.

Keep in mind that if your teen is still growing, her weight gain will need to keep pace with her growth. Kids who have had restrictive eating disorders often continue to lag in weight gain even after what seems like full recovery. In addition, teens who are finished growing should still be gaining weight over time, just more slowly. I recommend you continue to monitor weight; if weight drops you may need to make mini-interventions to increase weight using your previous tactics.

For Teens Who Are Moving Out

If your child has left the home or is leaving, oversight may be more difficult. In most cases, watching means having him weighed (often at a university medical center) at regular intervals. It also means observing and watching for changes in his state and eating behavior from afar. It is recommended that you continue to get weight checks every couple of weeks, and to stretch them out to every few months only when you're satisfied that your child is coping. This might be quite a bit later in the year, or even in the second year after he leaves. You will want to check in every few months during the first year your child is not living with you. As time passes, you can usually increase the length of time between weight checks and observations. For example, make a point to have an occasional meal with him and notice if there is any regression.

Although professionals trained in the earlier model of treatment for eating disorders might urge parents to back off once teens become adults, I believe that young adults with eating disorders still need their parents to help protect against relapse.

The Importance of Insight

While I think that insight is not required in the early stages of recovery, or indeed during most of the process, I do think that once a teen leaves the parents' home, insight becomes a critical part of relapse prevention. Kids who were treated for eating disorders at a younger age often do not seem to have much of a memory of ever having been ill. Parents can bear memory and remind the child of her vulnerability when she goes off to college or moves out on her own.

In the months before you entirely turn over the reins to your teen, or before your young adult moves out, talk to her about maintenance. Have conversations about the importance of being mindful of and guarding against relapse. Maintenance habits such as regular meals, eating enough dietary fat, managing stress, limiting exercise, and so on can be taught to a young adult so that she can implement the same strategies. Individual therapy for the young adult preparing to launch can be helpful and further buttress recovery skills. If you can, check out the therapist to make sure that he or she understands the continuing role of parents and doesn't shut you out of the process. I have also found that individual work with a dietitian experienced with eating disorders and FBT can be very valuable in preparing young adults for independent eating.

Kiko, from Michigan, shares her experience:

We took relapse prevention seriously, and it was two full years after the end of final treatment before she was truly ready to stand on her own against the remnants of the eating disorder without any backup monitoring. It was another year after that before I could truly breathe freely. An important part of this process has been for all of us to recognize warning signs of anxiety and the eating disorder that are not food related: rigid thinking expressed through being overly punctual, difficulty with decision making that shows up when shopping, and lack of flexibility when plans change. These early signs are a good reminder to ramp up mindful mental health care and full and adequate nutrition. Today she manages her eating disorder risk well and independently, and she is living the amazing and adventuresome life that she chose for herself—one the eating disorder never would have let her have.

ONLINE ACTIVITY 14: Relapse Prevention

To help you be prepared for relapse, download the worksheet from http://www.newharbinger.com/40439. You can then create a list of warning signs and high-risk situations to monitor.

What to Do If There Is a Lapse

If there is a lapse, first keep in mind that this is not a failure on the part of your teen, the treatment team, or you personally. Accept that relapse is often a step in the recovery process. It can be an opportunity to further strengthen recovery—you discover where the weak spots are and can shore them up. If your teen loses weight or resumes bingeing, purging, dieting, or overexercising, you are well prepared to return to the strategies that helped you help her recover in the first place.

This can be a scary place. Stay calm, but act right away! Many parents report that, having gone through FBT, they are well equipped to step back in and help their teen recover quickly from a lapse. Take charge and supervise just as you did the first time. The faster you catch your child after he falls off the bike and get him seated, the sooner he will be cruising around on his own again.

Here's how Molly, from Colorado, describes helping her daughter through a lapse:

> We are well and truly on the other side of relapse. She is back to eating everything. She is back to school and able to concentrate on homework. Her social life has amped up considerably, and she is managing the ups and downs of middle-school social interaction. There is also a return of those burgeoning flashes of "insight" every so often: she mentioned that she felt much better when she was in her "target range" and that it made sense for her to try to be there. She said, "Isn't it weird that I feel bad when I am skinnier and like the way I look when I weigh more?" Not like the "insight" is in any way fixed or stable...it comes and goes, and she mostly denies she has anorexia and can say without irony things like: "I haven't had a taste for hamburgers for a while, but I love them now."
>
> So, what changed? Weight! The kid is back to her range and exposure to three meals and three snacks a day.
>
> Relapse sucks but it really is a matter of "wash, rinse, repeat." We did a condensed version of what we did the first time around. I caught it very quickly this time and put all the controls back in right away.

Other Treatments

Finally, at this point, with your teen in recovery, you can see what symptoms remitted with the eating disorder and what remain. For example, if your teen's mood is not improved or he is showing signs of another mental health disorder, such as OCD or lingering body dysmorphia, it is at this point that you might want to obtain additional treatment for your teen.

Closing Thoughts

You have reached the end of the program on learning how to help your teen with an eating disorder.

What happens now? Your teen's development may lag behind her peers' due to the eating disorder. With time, she will catch up.

One of your tasks is to transition to a life no longer organized around helping your teen with an eating disorder. You can reclaim your life and once again attend to your own needs. If you're in a relationship, take some time to replenish the couple relationship, which may have taken a back seat while the focus was on saving your child's life.

I hope the resources and strategies I've provided have made the journey a little easier and more predictable. This process has required your focus, devotion, and love. Now that your teen's eating disorder is behind you, you can breathe a little easier.

The experience of parenting a child with an eating disorder can leave a residual anxiety about eating behaviors and potential relapse. Most parents report this will ease with time, and then you will be able to relish watching your teen or young adult go about building the wonderful life she is destined to live.

Acknowledgments

The case examples in this book are derived from multiple sources. Some are modified composites of families from my own practice who gave permission to use aspects of their stories. Others are from parents who were not my patients but graciously shared their stories and allowed me to use them. Some excerpts were originally posted on the Around the Dinner Table forum and are reprinted with permission.

Thank you to the following people who gave feedback on the book: Julie Anderson, PhD; Kristen Anderson, MA, LCSW; Marissa Corona, PhD; Gina Dimitropoulos, MSW, PhD; Elisheva Dorfman, LMFT; Tabitha Farrar; Kathleen Kara Fitzpatrick, PhD; Jennifer Gaudiani, MD; Melanie Jacob, RDN; Jennifer Johnson, MD; Leslie Kaplan, MD; Carol Moroney; Eva Musby; Lisa Olshefsky, PhD; Rebecka Peebles, MD; Renee Rienecke, PhD; Roxanne Rockwell, PhD; Jennifer Spengler; Alli Spotts-De Lazzer, LMFT, LPCC; and Therese Waterhous, PhD, RDN.

Thank you to Katie Grubiak, RDN, for her help with the nutrition components of this book. Special thanks to Rabbi Beth Lieberman, JD Ouellette, and Laura Collins Lyster-Mensh, who provided enthusiastic guidance, cheerleading, and moral support. Thanks to Kara Fitzpatrick for her wisdom and mentorship in teaching me much of what I know about FBT, and to G. Terence Wilson, PhD, for instilling the importance of evidence-based treatments and a love for eating disorders work. I am grateful to the National FBT Consultation Group for keeping me up to date and on my toes. Thanks to Families Empowered and Supporting the Treatment of Eating Disorders (F.E.A.S.T.) for their support. I have benefited greatly from the accounts of many families on the ATDT forum. Parents are my best teachers.

To all the families with whom I've worked, thank you for the opportunity. You inspire me as you heroically and unconditionally love and feed your children back to wellness. To numerous other colleagues and advocates in the eating disorder community (too numerous to name) who have supported me and this project—I appreciate your backing and guidance.

In a book celebrating the power of the family bond, I am forever grateful for my own family for their support and love. To my parents, Brenda and Richard Siegler, and my children, Henry, Rebecca, and Allison, thank you for your patience as I devoted my attention to this project. To my husband, Eric Muhlheim, you are not only the best husband, friend, and support I could imagine but also the most devoted editor—you can always help me find the perfect way to say exactly what I want to say. There is no one with whom I'd rather write a book than you.

Thank you to New Harbinger for giving me this amazing opportunity.

Bibliography

Arnold, C. 2013. *Decoding Anorexia: How Breakthroughs in Science Offer Hope for Eating Disorders*. New York: Routledge.

Brown, H. 2010. *Brave Girl Eating: A Family's Struggle with Anorexia*. New York: William Morrow.

Collins, L. 2014. *Eating with Your Anorexic: A Mother's Memoir*. Warrenton, Virginia: Biscotti Press.

Collins, L., and C. Bevan. 2015. *Throwing Starfish Across the Sea: A Pocket-Sized Care Package for the Parents of Someone with an Eating Disorder*. CreateSpace.

Katzman, D. K., R. Peebles, S. M. Sawyer, J. Lock, and D. Le Grange. 2013. "The Role of the Pediatrician in Family-Based Treatment for Adolescent Eating Disorders: Opportunities and Challenges." *The Journal of Adolescent Health: Official Publication of the Society for Adolescent Medicine* 53 (4): 433–40.

Le Grange, D., and J. Lock. 2007. *Treating Bulimia in Adolescents: A Family Based Approach*. New York: Guilford Press.

Le Grange, D., J. Lock, K. Loeb, and D. Nicholls. 2010. "Academy for Eating Disorders Position Paper: The Role of the Family in Eating Disorders." *International Journal of Eating Disorders* 43 (1): 1–5.

Lock, J., and Le Grange, D. 2015. *Help Your Teenager Beat an Eating Disorder*, 2nd ed. New York: Guilford Press.

Musby, E. 2014. *Anorexia and Other Eating Disorders: How to Help Your Child Eat Well and Be Well*. Aprica.

O'Toole, J. 2010. *Give Food A Chance: A New View on Childhood Eating Disorders*. Portland, Oregon: Perfectly Scientific Press.

White, H. J., E. Haycraft, S. Madden, P. Rhodes, J. Miskovic-Wheatley, A. Wallis, M. Kohn, and C. Meyer. 2017. "Parental Strategies Used in the Family Meal Session of Family-Based Treatment for Adolescent Anorexia Nervosa: Links with Treatment Outcomes." *International Journal of Eating Disorders* 50 (4): 433–36.

References

Academy for Eating Disorders (AED), Medical Care Standards Task Force. 2016. *Eating Disorders: Critical Points for Early Recognition and Medical Risk Management in the Care of Individuals with Eating Disorders.* 3rd ed. Reston, VA. Available at https://www.aedweb.org/learn/publications/medical-care-standards.

Accurso, E. C., A. C. Ciao, E. E. Fitzsimmons-Craft, J. D. Lock, and D. Le Grange. 2014. "Is Weight Gain Really a Catalyst for Broader Recovery?: The Impact of Weight Gain on Psychological Symptoms in the Treatment of Adolescent Anorexia Nervosa." *Behaviour Research and Therapy* 56: 1–6.

Ålgars, M., L. Huang, A. F. Von Holle, C. M. Peat, L. Thornton, P. Lichtenstein, and C. M. Bulik. 2014. "Binge Eating and Menstrual Dysfunction." *Journal of Psychosomatic Research* 76 (1): 19–22.

American Psychiatric Association. 2013. *Diagnostic and Statistical Manual of Mental Disorders*, 5th ed. Washington, DC.

Anderson, L. K., E. E. Reilly, L. Berner, C. E. Wierenga, M. D. Jones, T. A. Brown, W. H. Kaye, and A. Cusack. 2017. "Treating Eating Disorders at Higher Levels of Care: Overview and Challenges." *Current Psychiatry Reports* 19 (8): 48.

Arcelus, J., A. J. Mitchell, J. Wales, and S. Nielsen. 2011. "Mortality Rates in Patients with Anorexia Nervosa and Other Eating Disorders. A Meta-Analysis of 36 Studies." *Archives of General Psychiatry*, 68 (7), 724–31.

Bischoff-Grethe, A., D. McCurdy, E. Grenesko-Stevens, L. E. Irvine, A. Wagner, W. W. Yau, C. Fennema-Notestine, C. Wierenga,

J. L. Fudge, M. R. Delgado, and W. Kaye. 2013. "Altered Brain Response to Reward and Punishment in Adolescents with Anorexia Nervosa." *Psychiatry Research* 214 (3): 331–40.

Brandenburg, B. M. P., and A. E. Andersen. 2007. "Unintentional Onset of Anorexia Nervosa." *Eating and Weight Disorders* 12 (2): 97–100.

Bruch, H. 1978, 2001. *The Golden Cage: The Enigma of Anorexia Nervosa*. Cambridge, MA: Harvard University Press.

Campbell, K., and R. Peebles. 2014. "Eating Disorders in Children and Adolescents: State of the Art Review." *Pediatrics* 134 (3): 582–92.

Clausen, L. 2004. "Time Course of Symptom Remission in Eating Disorders." *The International Journal of Eating Disorders* 36 (3): 296–306.

Couturier, J., and J. Lock. 2006. "What Is Recovery in Adolescent Anorexia Nervosa?" The *International Journal of Eating Disorders* 39 (7): 550–55.

Eddy, K. T., D. J. Dorer, D. L. Franko, K. Tahilani, H. Thompson-Brenner, and D. B. Herzog. 2008. "Diagnostic Crossover in Anorexia Nervosa and Bulimia Nervosa: Implications for DSM-V." *American Journal of Psychiatry* 165 (2): 245–50.

Eddy, K. T., N. Tabri, J. J. Thomas, H. B. Murray, A. Keshaviah, E. Hastings, et al. 2017. "Recovery from Anorexia Nervosa and Bulimia Nervosa at 22-Year Follow-Up." *The Journal of Clinical Psychiatry* 78 (2): 184–89.

Fairburn, C. 2008. *Cognitive Behavior Therapy and Eating Disorders*. New York: Guilford Press.

Flament, M. F., H. Bissada, and W. Spettigue. 2012. "Evidence-Based Pharmacotherapy of Eating Disorders." *International Journal of Neuropsychopharmacology* 15 (2): 189–207.

Garber, A. K., S. M. Sawyer, N. H. Golden, A. S. Guarda, D. K. Katzman, M. R. Kohn, D. Le Grange, S. Madden, M. Whitelaw, and G. W. Redgrave. 2016. "A Systematic Review of

Approaches to Refeeding in Patients with Anorexia Nervosa." *International Journal of Eating Disorders* 49 (3): 293–310.

Garner, D. 1998. "The Effects of Starvation on Behavior: Implications for Dieting and Eating Disorders." *Healthy Weight Journal* 12 (5): 68–72.

Griffiths, S., S. B. Murray, and S. Touyz. 2013. "Disordered Eating and the Muscular Ideal." *Journal of Eating Disorders* 1 (April): 15.

Gull, W. 1873, published 1997. "V.-Anorexia Nervosa (Apepsia Hysterica, Anorexia Hysterica)." *Obesity Research* 5 (5): 498–502.

Harrison, M. E., N. Obeid, M. C. Y. Fu, and M. L. Norris. 2013. "Growth Curves in Short Supply: A Descriptive Study of the Availability and Utility of Growth Curve Data in Adolescents with Eating Disorders." *BMC Family Practice* 14: 134.

Hildebrandt, T., T. Bacow, M. Markella, and K. L. Loeb. 2012. "Anxiety in Anorexia Nervosa and Its Management Using Family-Based Treatment." *European Eating Disorders Review: The Journal of the Eating Disorders Association* 20 (1): e1–16.

Kaye, W. H., C. E. Wierenga, U. F. Bailer, A. N. Simmons, and A. Bischoff-Grethe. 2013. "Nothing Tastes as Good as Skinny Feels: The Neurobiology of Anorexia Nervosa." *Trends in Neurosciences* 36 (2): 110–20.

Keel, P. K., and T. F. Heatherton. 2010. "Weight Suppression Predicts Maintenance and Onset of Bulimic Syndromes at 10-Year Follow-Up." *Journal of Abnormal Psychology* 119 (2): 268–75.

Keys, A., J. Brozek, and A. Henschel. 1950. *The Biology of Human Starvation*. Minneapolis, MN: University of Minnesota Press.

Lebow, J., L. A. Sim, and E. C. Accurso. 2017. "Is There Clinical Consensus in Defining Weight Restoration for Adolescents with Anorexia Nervosa?" *Eating Disorders* Oct. 31: 1–8. DOI: 10.1080 /10640266.2017.1388664 [Epub ahead of print].

Le Grange, D., R. D. Crosby, P. J. Rathouz, and B. L. Leventhal. 2007. "A Randomized Controlled Comparison of Family-Based

Treatment and Supportive Psychotherapy for Adolescent Bulimia Nervosa." *Archives of General Psychiatry* 64 (9): 1,049–56.

Le Grange, D., J. Lock, W. S. Agras, A. Moye, S. W. Bryson, B. Jo, and H. C. Kraemer. 2012. "Moderators and Mediators of Remission in Family-Based Treatment and Adolescent Focused Therapy for Anorexia Nervosa." *Behaviour Research and Therapy* 50 (2): 85–92.

Lock, J., D. Le Grange, S. Agras, and C. Dare. 2001. *Treatment Manual for Anorexia Nervosa: A Family-Based Approach.* New York: Guilford.

Lock, J., W. S. Agras, S. Bryson, and H. C. Kraemer. 2005. "A Comparison of Short- and Long-Term Family Therapy for Adolescent Anorexia Nervosa." *Journal of the American Academy of Child & Adolescent Psychiatry* 44 (7): 632–39.

Lock, J., D. Le Grange, W. S. Agras, A. Moye, S. W. Bryson, and B. Jo. 2010. "Randomized Clinical Trial Comparing Family-Based Treatment to Adolescent Focused Individual Therapy for Adolescents with Anorexia Nervosa." *Archives of General Psychiatry* 67 (10): 1,025–32.

Lock, J. 2016. "Is Family-Based Treatment a Specific Therapy for Adolescents with Anorexia Nervosa?" In *Innovations in Family Therapy for Eating Disorders*, edited by S. Murray, L. K. Anderson, and L. Cohn. New York: Routledge.

Lyster-Mensh, L. C. 2011. "But It Would Kill Her!" *Laura's Soapbox* (blog). October 3. http://www.laurassoapbox.net/2011/10/but-it -would-kill-her.html.

Mahr, F., P. Farahmand, E. Bixler, R. Domen, E. Moser, T. Nadeem, et al. 2015. "A National Survey of Eating Disorder Training," *International Journal of Eating Disorders* 48 (4): 443–45.

Marzola, E., J. A. Nasser, S. A. Hashim, P. B. Shih, and W. H. Kaye. 2013. "Nutritional Rehabilitation in Anorexia Nervosa: Review of the Literature and Implications for Treatment." *BMC Psychiatry* 13: 290.

Mayer, L., B. T. Walsh, R. N. Pierson Jr., S. B. Heymsfield, D. Gallagher, J. Wang, et al. 2005. "Body Fat Redistribution after Weight Gain in Women with Anorexia Nervosa." *The American Journal of Clinical Nutrition* 81 (6): 1,286–91.

Mayer, L. E. S., D. A. Klein, E. Black, E. Attia, W. Shen, X. Mao, et al. 2009. "Adipose Tissue Distribution after Weight Restoration and Weight Maintenance in Women with Anorexia Nervosa." *The American Journal of Clinical Nutrition* 90 (5): 1,132–37.

Milos, G., C. Kuenzli, C. M. Soelch, S. Schumacher, H. Moergeli, and C. Mueller-Pfeiffer. 2013. "How Much Should I Eat? Estimation of Meal Portions in Anorexia Nervosa." *Appetite* 63: 42–7.

Murray, S. B., S. Griffiths, and D. Le Grange. 2014. "The Role of Collegial Alliance in Family-Based Treatment of Adolescent Anorexia Nervosa: A Pilot Study." *International Journal of Eating Disorders* 47 (4): 418–21.

O'Toole, J. 2013. "The Very Young Child With Anorexia." Kartini Clinic Blog. October 31, https://www.kartiniclinic.com/blog/post/the-very-young-child-with-anorexia

Parks, E., L. K. Anderson, and A. Cusack. 2016. "Adolescent Impressions of Family Involvement in the Treatment of Eating Disorders." In *Innovations in Family Therapy for Eating Disorders*, edited by S. Murray, L. K. Anderson, and L. Cohn. New York: Routledge.

Schaefer, J., and T. T. Rutledge. 2004. *Life Without Ed: How One Woman Declared Independence from Her Eating Disorder and How You Can Too.* New York: McGraw-Hill.

Schebendach, J., L. E. S. Mayer, M. J. Devlin, E. Attia, and B. T. Walsh. 2012. "Dietary Energy Density and Diet Variety as Risk Factors for Relapse in Anorexia Nervosa: A Replication." *The International Journal of Eating Disorders* 45 (1): 79–84.

Spotts-De Lazzer, A., and L. Muhlheim. 2016. "Eating Disorders and Scope of Competence for Outpatient Psychotherapists." *Practice Innovations* 1 (2): 89–104.

Victorian Centre of Excellence in Eating Disorders. 2016. Unpublished data.

Wallis, A., P. Rhodes, L. Dawson, J. Miskovic-Wheatley, S. Madden, and S. Touyz. 2017. "Relational Containment: Exploring the Effect of Family-Based Treatment for Anorexia on Familial Relationships." *Journal of Eating Disorders* 5: 27.

Walsh, T., J. Yager, and D. Solomon. 2013. "Anorexia Nervosa in Adults: Pharmacotherapy." UpToDate.

White, H. J., E. Haycraft, S. Madden, P. Rhodes, J. Miskovic-Wheatley, A. Wallis, M. Kohn, and C. Meyer. 2015. "How Do Parents of Adolescent Patients with Anorexia Nervosa Interact with Their Child at Mealtimes? A Study of Parental Strategies Used in the Family Meal Session of Family-Based Treatment." *International Journal of Eating Disorders* 48 (1): 72–80.

Yager, J., M. J. Devlin, K. A. Halmi, D. B. Herzog, J. E. Mitchell, P. Powers, K. Zerbe. 2012. *Guideline Watch: Practice Guideline for the Treatment of Patients with Eating Disorders*, 3rd. ed. Washington, D.C.: American Psychological Association.

Zunker, C., C. B. Peterson, R. D. Crosby, L. Cao, S. G. Engel, J. E. Mitchell, and S.A. Wonderlich. 2011. "Ecological Momentary Assessment of Bulimia Nervosa: Does Dietary Restriction Predict Binge Eating?" *Behaviour Research and Therapy* 49 (10): 714–717.

Lauren Muhlheim, PsyD is a clinical psychologist and eating disorders specialist. Muhlheim trained at the Rutgers Eating Disorder Clinic, and is certified in family-based treatment (FBT) by the Training Institute for Child and Adolescent Eating Disorders. She is certified as an eating disorder specialist (CEDS) through the International Association of Eating Disorders Professionals (IAEDP), and has worked in a variety of settings, including an obesity research center, inpatient hospitals, outpatient clinics, group homes, and in private practice where more than 80 percent of her patients present with eating disorders.

Muhlheim conducts workshops and seminars for parents, treatment professionals, graduate students in psychology, and psychiatry residents approximately six times per year. She has her own website and blog, is the eating disorders expert for www.verywell.com, and is clinical director for the eating disorder information website, Mirror-Mirror Eating Disorder (www.mirror-mirror.org/eatdis.htm). She's affiliated with a number of eating disorder and psychology organizations, and is very active on social media. She has built a solid professional platform around eating disorder recovery using FBT. Currently, she is director of Eating Disorder Therapy LA, a multidisciplinary, specialized outpatient eating disorder practice in the heart of Los Angeles, CA.

Foreword writer **Laura Collins Lyster-Mensh** is a writer from Virginia who became an activist for improved eating disorder treatment after the recovery of her teen daughter from anorexia. Her book, *Eating with Your Anorexic*, is a memoir of her family's experience. She has written two books on eating disorders, a memoir, and one book of fiction. She has helped found three eating disorder organizations, and currently serves as outreach director for one of them: F.E.A.S.T., the only international organization for parents of eating disorder patients. She is also owner of Circum Mensam LLC, where she is a consultant and educator. She has been an invited speaker for many organizations. Collins is also frequently interviewed by the media, including *The Washington Post*, *The New York Times*, BBC News, *The Wall Street Journal*, *Newsweek*, NPR, and the *Los Angeles Times*.

Real change *is* possible

For more than forty-five years, New Harbinger has published proven-effective self-help books and pioneering workbooks to help readers of all ages and backgrounds improve mental health and well-being, and achieve lasting personal growth. In addition, our spirituality books offer profound guidance for deepening awareness and cultivating healing, self-discovery, and fulfillment.

Founded by psychologist Matthew McKay and Patrick Fanning, New Harbinger is proud to be an independent, employee-owned company. Our books reflect our core values of integrity, innovation, commitment, sustainability, compassion, and trust. Written by leaders in the field and recommended by therapists worldwide, New Harbinger books are practical, accessible, and provide real tools for real change.

 **newharbinger**publications

MORE BOOKS *from*
NEW HARBINGER PUBLICATIONS

Register your **new harbinger** titles for additional benefits!

When you register your **new harbinger** title—purchased in any format, from any source—you get access to benefits like the following:

- Downloadable accessories like printable worksheets and extra content

- Instructional videos and audio files

- Information about updates, corrections, and new editions

Not every title has accessories, but we're adding new material all the time.

Access free accessories in 3 easy steps:

1. Sign in at NewHarbinger.com (or **register** to create an account).

2. Click on **register a book**. Search for your title and click the **register** button when it appears.

3. Click on the **book cover or title** to go to its details page. Click on **accessories** to view and access files.

That's all there is to it!

If you need help, visit:

NewHarbinger.com/accessories

new harbinger
CELEBRATING
40 YEARS